ANGLICAN RELIGIOUS LIFE

ANGLICAN RELIGIOUS LIFE

A well kept secret?

EDITED BY

Nicolas Stebbing CR

DOMINICAN PUBLICATIONS

First published (2003) by
Dominican Publications
42 Parnell Square
Dublin 1

ISBN 1-871552-83-4

British Library Cataloguing in Publications Data.
A catalogue record for this book is available
from the British Library.

Cover design by David Cooke

Printed in Ireland by
The Leinster Leader Ltd
Naas, Co. Kildare.

Contents

Introduction

NICOLAS CR

'*Are* there nuns and monks in the Anglican Church?' 160 years after Marian Hughes made her profession as the first Anglican nun since the Reformation, the question is still asked. It is fair to say that the majority of Anglicans assume all monks and nuns are Roman Catholics and are amazed to find that some of us are Anglicans. Archbishop George Carey once described the religious life [1] as 'the best kept secret in the Church of England'.

In many ways that is how it should be. There is something contradictory, even distasteful, about high profile monks and nuns. Much of the life will always be unknown, unsung and misunderstood. Religious life began in the desert and its healthiest forms are often to be found on the margins, on the edge where life is precarious and not much is known. Publicity is a dangerous beast and we should not worry about whether people know we exist, or even know very much about what we do.

And yet, the recovery of the religious life in the Anglican Church has been a great story of a gift from God. God has been very good to us, and many of those who pioneered this life were great and holy people. It is right that people should know about the goodness and the activity of God. This we want to celebrate. Moreover, Anglican religious life, at least in the West, is facing a critical time. We need prayers; we need ideas; we need to encourage each other. Those of us who have joined together in producing this book have found it an

---

1. Religious life is the term commonly used to describe the life lived under the traditional vows – either of poverty, chastity and obedience, or of obedience, stability and conversion of life. Technically monks and nuns are those who live the monastic life, and most other religious are called apostolic or active religious. This distinction is not much used amongst Anglicans.

exciting and invigorating exercise. As religious life now enters a time of some confusion, doubt and revision, we need to be encouraged by what God, through his people, has done in the past.

Almost everyone with any knowledge of English history knows that Henry VIII closed down all the monasteries of monks and nuns in England and Wales during the 1530s. Apart from a brief revival under Mary Tudor, no religious life existed in the Church of England for three centuries. In the early seventeenth century Nicholas Ferrar and his family tried to live a form of religious life at Little Gidding, but that came to an end during the Civil War.

However, in the early nineteenth century people began to wish that at least something like the Catholic Sisters of Mercy might come into existence in order to engage in the work of teaching, nursing and care for the poor. Such hopes remained unfulfilled until the vision of the Oxford Movement encouraged a particular response to God – a longing for life with him, a longing to give oneself to God in a life of dedicated service, and to do so in a way that made possible a full liturgical and sacramental life, such as was not available in the parish churches. So Marian Hughes made her profession in 1841, but she was not able then to start a community. The first community was the Park Village Sisterhood in 1845. This later amalgamated with the Society of the Holy Trinity founded (in 1848) by the redoubtable Lydia Sellon in Devonport, and became Ascot Priory.

Meanwhile in Wantage the vicar, William Butler, founded the Community of St Mary the Virgin, a community which, though in the end larger than most, became fairly typical of Anglican sisterhoods. They had from the start a commitment to a fairly rigorous devotional life coupled with a considerable amount of pastoral work, teaching, nursing in the homes round about and looking after 'fallen' women. In this they followed the pattern of Roman Catholic religious orders, chiefly in France.

During the next twenty years a large number of sisterhoods were founded and some grew spectacularly as women came to discover the romance of the religious life, the opportunity to serve the Church or

the chance to do really satisfying work amongst the poor.[2]
It was not until 1865, however, that the first community of men was
founded. This was the Society of St John the Evangelist, founded by
Fr Richard Meux Benson. Again, this set the pattern for some other
foundations – largely of priests, with a commitment to say (or sing) the
Anglican offices of Matins and Evensong, enriched with other Offices
from Roman Catholic sources, and yet also to engage in priestly
ministry, often of an evangelistic kind. The Society of St John the
Evangelist was followed in 1892 by the Community of the Resurrection and, in 1894, by the Society of the Sacred Mission. These two
communities both soon became considerably involved in training
young men for the priesthood, particularly those young men from
poor backgrounds who could not finance their own training, as future
priests were expected to do in those days. For these men's communities, the work, apart from life in community, revolved around parish
missions, the giving of retreats, a ministry of Confession and spiritual
direction and, with the last two, teaching theology. Soon all three were
doing mission work in Africa and India, generally with help from
Sisters.

During the latter years of the nineteenth century, various attempts
were made to begin Franciscan or Benedictine communities; but for
reasons usually concerned with the instability of the founding brethren, or their eccentric ideas of religious life, these did not persevere.
In the end a Franciscan community, the Society of the Divine Compassion, came into existence which, through a fairly complicated
route [3] eventually joined with other Franciscan bodies in the Society
of St Francis, in the twentieth century. Likewise, a reasonably stable
Benedictine house at Caldey Island gave hopes of the revival of
Benedictine life. Most of this Community became Roman Catholic in
1913; but those left as Anglicans provided the nucleus of what
evolved into Nashdom (now Elmore) Abbey.

Meanwhile, contemplative life for women had evolved in several

---

2. Susan Mumm's *Stolen Daughters, Virgin Mothers* is a wonderful description of this era.
3. See P. Dunstan, *This Poor Sort.*

forms, Benedictines (at West Malling), Augustinians (the Society of the Precious Blood at Burnham Abbey), the Society of the Sacred Cross at Tymawr, and the Sisters of the Love of God at Fairacres were only some of the communities that provided the full contemplative life, usually strictly enclosed, for women.[4]

The nineteenth century was a great century of expansion for the British Empire, and particularly for the Church of England which rapidly found itself the centre of an expanding Anglican Communion. This led to an explosion of missionary concern. Religious life inevitably found itself caught up in this expansion, either as part of the Oxford Movement, or of the missionary impulse. So communities found their way to the United States of America, to South Africa, Australia, Central Africa, India and elsewhere. Indigenous communities were also founded in these countries. As a missionary story, it has been a splendid era. As a manifestation of religious life, the story is somewhat more problematic. Few of the English Orders who went out as missionaries now flourish in other parts of the world; but many have been the communities founded in surprising places, like Melanesia, which have grown beyond all expectations.

And so to the present day and the future, which, to a large degree, is what this book is concerned with. In England the years since the 1960s have been a confusing time for religious communities. Almost all are now much smaller and, in company with our Roman Catholic sisters and brothers, have fewer novices. Much change has been tried. Some seems to have worked well. Other change has seemed to go nowhere. The confusing world of the postmodern seems to be the world we must make our home in, with little idea of how it will develop. Yet a glance through the *Anglican Religious Communities Year Book* shows amazing changes in the wider Anglican Communion. The Community of the Holy Name in Southern Africa, the Community of St Mary in Tanzania, the Melanesian Brotherhood in

---

4. The communities whose names are given in this essay are only a small selection of those which exist, or have existed. Peter Anson's *Call of the Cloister* and the current *Anglican Religious Life Year Book* are good sources of additional information. See also Bibliography.

the Solomon Islands, show a continuous growth and vigour. Clearly there are many stories to be told and the manner in which God continues to work continues to surprise us.

The essays begin with an overview by a Church historian. Petà Dunstan looks at some of the factors in the mid nineteenth century which, under God, inspired this rebirth of religious life and contributed to the identity which Anglican religious now find is theirs. Hilary then picks up the attempts communities have made to respond to the radical change of the 1960s, most particularly the Vatican Council. Nicolas describes both the glory and the problems of the religious community in a foreign mission, and so highlights the difficulties we often have in relating pastoral work to religious life. Annaliese shows how her community has responded to some of the most intractable social problems of urban life, by getting deeply involved. Richard brings the first section to a close with a description of the amazing response which young Melanesian men have made to the challenge of living common life as a basis to mission.

In the second section, Stephanie Thérèse reflects on the nature of the vowed life, which lies at the heart of our response, and the vows which need to be engaged with constantly as we try to live our life to the full. Gillian Ruth takes the experience of the Dark Night, as found particularly in John of the Cross, and relates it to the experience most of us now have of vulnerability in an insecure present and uncertain future. Alistair, as a clinical psychologist, looks at the way in which brothers and sisters need to grow to maturity in the complex world of a religious community. Nicolas then tries to describe what prayer can be, and maybe even is, though it may not often seem like it; and Emma brings us back to the heart of God where our vocation begins and lives and hopes to find its completion.

We would like this book to have told the whole story of Anglican religious life and to have produced clear indications of where it is going and what would be the most profitable paths down which we could go. In fact it quickly became clear that the story was too big to be told in one book, at least by us. And the future is far too uncertain for us to do more than guess at what it will hold. So we have simply each written about what most interests us. Each essay has been discussed at length by the group and we have been delighted to find that a large amount of agreement was to be found amongst us, and an enthusiasm for each other's expression of the religious life, even though we differ very much in our individual vocations. Our hope is that the range of subjects covered by the essayists will show that much is happening, under the grace of God and that others, both in the Anglican religious life and outside it, will be encouraged by our work to push the roads out a little further into that unknown future, which sometimes looks so dark, so confusing, so frightening, even so bleak and yet, in the end, is the place we will find God.

It is a place which is 'on the edge'. Being on the edge can be very lonely, very isolated. One can feel forgotten or ignored. Or it can be an edge which no one else has explored, a place of excitement and adventure. It may be an edge which feels very precarious, with nothing around it and the great danger of falling off. It can be a place of freedom, where conventions have been left behind and the air is fresh and clear. Religious life almost always begins as a venture of faith, a gamble, a walking out into the unknown. Yet it can easily lose that sense of adventure and becomes secure, institutionalised and deeply conservative. This too has its value in giving depth and stability to the Church, but the security can easily stagnate and become a state which is hostile to the freedom of God. As we have talked through our essays, we have found many edges – some exciting, some alarming. We invite our readers, and especially our fellow religious, to come with us to some of these edges and see what may be found.

ONE

Evolving Identity
in Anglican Religious Life

PETÀ DUNSTAN

Every movement is coloured by the historical context in which it arises. The revival of religious communities within the Church of England in the 1840s, and then in other parts of the Anglican Communion in the following decades, is no exception. Both the timing of the revival, and the subsequent evolution of the identity of Anglican religious communities, can be associated with particular sociological and theological factors. Initially, communities were shaped by the challenges they faced in the early decades of their development. This created an influential identity or 'blueprint' which established a pattern for later foundations, particularly so because this 'identity' appeared to deliver vocations, achievements and a gradual acceptance both inside and outside the Church.

The period 1845–1914 was one of phenomenal growth for Anglican communities. Starting with groups of sisters, serving the poor through nursing, orphanages, schools and other social projects, the enthusiasm for communities grew steadily. By the end of the nineteenth century, it is estimated that there were over 2,000 Anglican religious in Great Britain alone. Foundations began in North America, Africa and Australasia, some founded from Britain, others locally, and amongst men as well as women. Despite the initial hostility, communities gradually began to be tolerated and then gain a measure of approval from both Church authorities and wider society.

In the twentieth century that approval grew. Some male religious were consecrated as bishops, others served on Church advisory bodies, and in 1935 a more formal recognition was given in the creation of the Advisory Council, a body made up of bishops and religious to advise the archbishops on community issues. By the 1950s, the very names 'Mirfield', 'Cowley', 'Wantage' – the locations of community mother houses – resonated with their own authority and as watch words for certain standards of service and activities within and outside the Church. Religious life might still have been treated with suspicion by some evangelical Anglicans, but elsewhere in the Church members of communities commanded a respect and authority never afforded to the founding generation. The qualities and practices required to establish and maintain communities in mid-Victorian society were now enshrined as 'the religious life' among Anglicans.

However, there was a decline in vocations in the second half of the twentieth century, parallel with a closing of the large corporate religious institutions as the State began to take over the educational, health and social services which communities had provided. The Church itself also saw a drop in membership and practice, requiring a radical reappraisal of its role. In a new era, the nineteenth-century model of religious life seemed no longer appropriate. The story of Anglican religious in more recent decades therefore has been one of attempts to emerge from beneath the Victorian 'prototype' and express in a different context the underlying values at the heart of the life.

Reflecting upon the historical identity of Anglican religious life can be an aid to understanding this complex process, and this essay briefly attempts such an approach. Not all factors relate to every community, but an overview can be helpful in mapping the background to the contemporary challenges which religious life faces. First, we must consider in more detail the factors which allowed for the foundation of such a profusion of communities in the Victorian period.

RE-EMERGENCE

This reflection on identity begins with the reasons why religious life amongst Anglicans re-emerged in the 1840s. The first was a theological shift in the Church of England following the campaign of a group of Oxford dons, commonly called the Tractarians, who wished to reawaken the Church of England to its Catholic heritage. In the early 1830s, these Tractarian leaders began their campaign against the spread of liberalism in the Church, both the political liberalism which was leading to state interference in ecclesiastical affairs, and the liberalism of the new theological ideas and methodology (mainly from Germany) which was gaining credibility in academic debate. In order to protect the Church from this threat, these Churchmen had to do more than protest and be reactive: they had to provide a path which was an alternative to liberalism. This they did by looking back to Patristic theology and the tradition of the Church. The theology of the Fathers was heavily influenced by monasticism and its insights, and the significance of religious life became clear to the Tractarians. From this perspective, the re-establishment of religious communities was essential for the spiritual health of the Church, and the Oxford Movement in its widest sense encouraged this.

The second reason was political. For generations, Roman Catholicism had been linked politically with Britain's enemies (primarily France and Spain) and therefore anything associated with 'Romanism' was suspect. The cry of 'No Popery' was a potent one. As religious life was intimately connected in the public mind with Roman Catholicism, hostility to the idea of communities within the Church of England was fierce.

But in the 1790s, the French Revolution raised an enemy far worse than Roman Catholicism. The radical leaders of France and their ideas were such a danger in the minds of the British ruling class that Roman Catholic priests and monks and nuns who fled from them were welcomed to Great Britain as refugees. The enemy's enemy became a friend. Ironically, the old cry of 'No Popery' would be revived at the time of the Tractarians, but the shift of opinion in parts of the Church of England had already happened. Religious life was no longer so strongly shackled by the old taboos.

Third comes a cultural reason. The Romantic Movement had produced, both in academia and more generally in British culture, a rejection of the rationalism of the eighteenth century ('the Age of Reason') and in its wake came an admiration for the pre-Reformation era. Medieval Gothic became fashionable; and monks and nuns became a part of the medieval imagery which appealed to a large section of Victorian opinion. Although the favour shown to the externals of religious life as a consequence was not particularly deep or comprehending of its purposes, it nevertheless helped to make the revival of real communities less threatening. The concept of monastic life may have remained eccentric to many, but it was no longer alien.

Finally, there was a social reason, perhaps the most significant of all. The Industrial Revolution – and the accompanying increase in population – had produced by the 1840s an urban poverty on a scale previously unimagined. The visibility of the squalor and hardship which the new capitalist economy created was a grave challenge not just to governments but to the Church. For the Church had the pastoral responsibility for all those living in the new city slums, which had grown quickly and haphazardly. Calls for sisterhoods to help the clergy to respond to the pastoral crisis predated the Tractarian movement. With the other factors already mentioned, this need overcame the prejudices, and the movement to found communities developed rapidly. In founding hospitals and schools and providing other services to the poor and destitute, religious communities offered on behalf of the Church one powerful response to the harsh economic realities of contemporary society.

THE FORGING OF CORPORATE IDENTITY

There are many factors relevant to the development of any particular community, but, from the reasons given above, we can consider three consequences which broadly influenced most Anglican foundations.

1. Achievement and acceptance through works

The acceptance by Anglicans of their own religious communities was bound up with the work these communities undertook. The heroic and self-sacrificial action of sisters, whether in cholera epidemics, slum parishes or in caring for orphans and the elderly poor, overcame the suspicions evident in the earliest years of the revival. The initial failure of attempts to found men's communities was partly because of the problems they had in emulating the nursing and educational services which sisters were providing. Men did not need to be religious to do pastoral or teaching work, as they could be parish priests and curates, whilst activities like nursing were regarded as female occupations.

Not only was the social work seen as the justification for religious life, but the institutions which communities created – schools, hospitals, orphanages, refuges – were the source of their public achievement and recognition. The valuable services these institutions provided were the communities' first-line defence against criticism from both inside and outside the Church. A fierce Evangelical might rage against the vows and traditions of religious communities, but could not credibly attack the work they did. On an intellectual level, one of the strongest criticisms of the religious life was that monks and nuns were 'parasites' on society. This was the kernel of much anti-Catholic rhetoric against communities, but it was hollow when pitted against the achievements of Anglican religious in the nineteenth century.

Being 'useful to society' became, then, a deeply-embedded aspect of Anglican identity, and loyalty to the founder or foundress's vision maintained it. It became an essential ingredient of new foundations. This was equally true in other parts of the Anglican Communion besides Great Britain.

The emergence of cloistered contemplative communities was hampered by this need to demonstrate their 'worth'. Some, like the Benedictine community now at Malling Abbey, and the Servants of Christ, evolved from 'active' communities. Others, like the Society of the Holy Trinity, had a group of 'contemplatives' in one house of the order whilst other sisters were engaged in social work. In 1906 came the establishment of a community specifically for the contemplative vocation: the Sisters of the Love of God, in Oxford. Those communities which did emerge in the twentieth century as enclosed did so because they remained relatively unknown and unpublicised; they also had powerful protectors within the Church, often a male 'active' community, to shield them. As late as the 1940s, when the Community of St Clare was founded as the Second Order of the Society of St Francis, it was regarded by many as praying for the First Order brothers; their prayer was a 'work' to support the social work of their brethren. Amongst men' s communities, the Benedictine community at Pershore, which was not intended as an order founded for social work, nevertheless felt obliged in the early 1920s to send brothers to Africa to serve the Church's missionary work when it was still numerically weak and its members young in the religious life.

Given the historical context in which most communities were founded, it is understandable that their 'success' was judged, both inside and outside the Church, principally by 'works'. As such, the strength and success of the revival of religious life among Anglicans became for many inextricably linked with the pattern of those achievements. Anglican religious life was thus given a particular identity, one held strongly both by members of communities and, equally importantly, by their supporters in the Church.

2. A Gothic emphasis on piety and externals

The founding of communities in an age when the neo-Gothic fashion was at its height had the consequence that most Anglican communities were associated with a Gothic piety. Many of their purpose-built convents were designed in this fashion, and these buildings were permanent features of their life. However many small branch houses a community might have, the 'Mother house' was usually a solid Victorian mansion of large proportion with pointed windows and turrets or castellations. Even those of a simpler design were like fortresses, the 'walls' of the popular view of convents, imposing and somewhat secretive. Some buildings were classics of their type, others were closer to medieval pastiches. It might be judged that some were as much the fulfilment of the fantasies of the communities' benefactors, who paid for their construction, as of the religious themselves. Whether good or bad architecturally, these buildings defined communities, and continued to place them in a particular time and context long after that era was gone.

Similarly, some communities evolved elaborate and voluminous habits, which bathed their wearers in an aura of mystery. Some sisters even had 'trains' to the skirts of their habits, justified by saying that a sister would not then show the back of her shoes when she had to lean over a bed in a hospital ward. Even amongst communities for men, a similar concern for Gothic externals could appear – one needs only to look at photographs of the Caldey Island monks in the early 1900s to recognise this. Some of these poses were exaggerated, to pander to the image which many outside the communities envisioned, a fantasy re-creation of how they believed medieval monks and nuns had lived.

Much of it was nonsense: it neither reflected how religious had lived centuries before nor how they lived in the nineteenth century. But those who adopted the Gothic extras were those who gained most publicity (or, some might judge, notoriety) and the support, financial as well as moral, of some of the most generous benefactors. Not that these accoutrements were of themselves injurious to religious life, but, again, they were a factor in placing Anglican religious life in a particular context. As secular clothing developed new and simpler fashions, especially for women, and architecture embraced less florid lines, the fuss of Gothic details linked religious with a bygone age.

In worship too, the introduction of ceremonial and what were termed 'full Catholic privileges', an issue which created argument in the Church of England and beyond, also involved communities. Many convent chapels adopted – sometimes even secretly – practices and ornaments which were controversial in the context of the Victorian Church. In addition, the very taking of vows was a source of dissension with the local bishop in some dioceses until well into the twentieth century. Worship in some communities became elaborate with many 'frills' (as they were popularly termed), and the resulting liturgical splendour was as much a part of the Gothic revival as the architectural flourishes of the new convent buildings. The struggle for Catholic worship made those liturgical forms a significant element in corporate identity.

Many Anglican communities therefore found both the formation of their way of life, and the expectations of those outside it, increasingly influenced by all these Gothic trappings. Potential recruits arrived – even in Victorian times – with an image of life in community derived largely from a fantasy of medieval religious life. Outside the convents, similar caricatures of what being a religious meant, were hard to dispel. Religious found themselves saddled in the public mind with an identity which ran counter to their evolving work and ethos. Even if the religious changed, the expectations of both their supporters and critics frequently did not.

3. Rebellion and struggle

The other factor in defining identity for Anglican religious was the result of their early struggle for acceptance. The title of Donald Allchin's well-known book about the beginnings of the revival sums this up: *The Silent Rebellion.* Many of those who pioneered community life in the 1840s, 1850s and 1860s saw themselves as essentially counter-cultural. They were defying the lack of sympathy for religious life within society as a whole, and also defying the prevailing attitude amongst bishops and the authorities of the Church of England. Significantly, religious life was not regulated systematically among Anglicans as it was for Roman Catholics. Indeed, even the formal mechanisms for consultation between Anglican communities and bishops were not ordered until well into the twentieth century. Thus, the early founders were in practice able to develop communities in keeping with their own personal vision. For many of these individuals, their vocation had also led them into defiance of the wishes of their families. The religious who pioneered Anglican foundations were therefore courageous individuals, unafraid of criticism, strong enough to resist social and personal pressure. The faint-hearted soon gave up; those who persevered were self-sufficient and single-minded.

In consequence, many early Anglican foundations were vigorously independent in spirit, and suspicious of external influence. They had little to do with each other and there was little open co-operation between communities, even where there might be sympathy. The spirit of the founder that animated his or her community, and united the members as a group, was also one of determined resistance to outside interference. Standing up to opposition was part of the attractive adventure of the life. Criticism could be dismissed as partisan propaganda. As a result, superiors could become very powerful, and 'personal rule' was not uncommon. All this held the danger of making communities inward-looking and reliant on particular individuals, creators of their own tradition rather than seeing themselves as a part of a centuries-old tradition stretching back to the earliest years of the Church as a whole.

When times changed and a renewal of vision was required, it was hard for leaders to take notice of advice from 'outside'. The experience of years of criticism and the policy of ignoring it, handed down from the founders, fostered within many community members an unwillingness to take note of opinions from outside. Change could be seen as betrayal and a weakening of community cohesion in an uncertain world. Ironically, then, the spirit of rebellion had ossified into a policy of conservation. What was once radical and new was now 'tradition' and unalterable. The founding spirit of defiance and independence became the same spirit which resisted change.

THE CRISIS OF THIS IDENTITY

We have identified three factors, then, in the corporate identity of Anglican religious: a strong emphasis on 'works'; an attachment to the neo-Gothic in worship and externals; a spirit of independence and resistance to change from outside. None of these aspects of identity were in themselves detrimental or misguided. Indeed, they were the bedrock of the 'success' of the revival of religious life. They anchored the early communities and helped them grow rapidly, even in a hostile cultural climate. They were therefore commendable in, and appropriate to, the times in which they were forged. Nevertheless, it was the very significance and value of these factors which made them difficult to modify or build upon in a later era.

The crisis for Anglican religious communities began around the

First World War. The effects of that conflict on social attitudes and expectations were enormous. Many trends, such as the emancipation of women and the decline in Church attendance, which had emerged before the war, were now accelerated. The gradual incursion of the State into areas of education and health provision was also deepening. For example, in Britain, 1919 saw the beginning of State Registered Nurses. Nursing had been established as a profession by the work of religious communities – indeed, much of its structure and nomenclature still echo today the traditions of religious life. After 1919, women who wished to follow this vocation could do so easily and respectably without joining a religious community.

Such developments began the decline in religious vocations to 'active' communities, and, as the decades passed, communities found it increasingly difficult to staff their institutions. At first, they coped by employing 'seculars', but eventually most of their schools and hospitals either had to close or else be handed over to the State or another authority. The plethora of new government regulations demanding a range of standards in buildings, methods and the training of personnel, added to the pressures. By the 1960s, most communities could no longer sustain the running of institutions.

The closure of their institutions by religious was also the product of new social attitudes. Corporate achievement was no longer the most significant goal. The first half of the twentieth century had been a time for organisations and uniforms and being part of a team. Not just religious communities, but organisations such as the Boy Scouts and the Mothers' Union flourished. Joining a group and wearing a uniform were encouraged. Political parties were not immune, but the results were catastrophic: fascists and communists between them were instrumental in destroying democracy throughout much of Europe. Even on the edge of the continent, Great Britain had its Black Shirts and 'Reds', and fighting in the streets. Overwhelming group identities in politics led to rivalry and aggression, and ultimately into world war.

In contrast, the post-1945 era would turn its back on such identities and, instead, encourage individualism. Aided by the new insights of psychology, the new culture emphasised personal achievement and fulfilment. The effect on communities was wide-ranging. Many brothers and sisters became aware of the need for this personal achievement. It led to some fragmentation in community life. Individual ministries, religious living alone on 'detached service', and less attachment to the symbols of common identity such as the habit, became common.

In such a world, the corporate worship which had defined the communities as much as their institutions also became a matter of controversy. As the Church embraced liturgical reform in the 1960s, many communities found it hard to adapt. Retrospectively, some of the disagreements might seem unimportant, but if the issue of identity is fully appreciated, the anguish of some religious can be understood. Much of what was abandoned had been at the heart of what they had been taught, sometimes by those who had struggled so valiantly to establish the rituals in the first place. What to some might seem like 'extras' were to others the symbol of all that they believed and had sacrificed so much to follow. It might be an outmoded identity for some, but to those who cherished these traditions, they were integral to their identity, and irreplaceable components of religious life. Equally, changing or abandoning habits and/or moving from much-loved buildings were bewildering and disheartening decisions. The changes split communities, and some religious left the life because of too much change or else too little. Some leaders were left drained and despairing in their efforts to reach a consensus amidst the confusion.

Finally, we must consider what happened to the spirit of rebellion. As the Catholic movement became increasingly strong amongst Anglicans, reaching its greatest influence between the two world wars, religious life seemed less and less like a protest. Ironically, the very 'success' of religious, which brought increased respect, resulted in their being more and more closely associated with authority. Some religious became bishops, others began running parishes. The identification of the nun's habit with the headmistress, hospital matron,

Sunday school instructor or other authority figure became common-place. This authority of religious was regularly exercised over chil-dren, so that even those who ceased to be church-goers as adults retained this image in their minds. The leaders of communities were shown a reverence, even held in awe, sometimes bowed and curtseyed to like monarchs. The very terms, like 'Father Superior' or 'Mother General', had a resonance way beyond the communities they served. By the middle of the twentieth century, religious were no longer at the margins, mavericks or eccentrics, but, willingly or not, they had become linked with the structures of power in the Church. No longer at odds with bishops and clergy, as so frequently in Victorian times, it could be argued that they had become 'clericalised' in popular culture.

In this context, to join a religious community was hardly to rebel. On the contrary, a vocation could be seen in the opposite light, as an act of conformity to tradition. It came to appear counter to the increasingly popular notions of 'freedom' and 'individuality'. If you wished to rebel, you 'did your own thing': you did not join a group with a uniform. The true freedom of the vows was thus obscured by the popular connection of religious life with the past. To wear a habit and live in a large Victorian building under a set of 'old-fashioned' rules appeared to a post-1945 generation as 'living in the past'. The truth of religious life was far removed from such ideas, but this was the identification which clung.

The historical pillars of the identity of many Anglican religious which this essay has considered, therefore collapsed. The process began slowly after 1918 and then accelerated in the post-1945 period. Corporate identity through institutional works and achievements, through a Gothic style of piety and worship, and the spirit of rebellion was no longer possible. Vocations declined, and communities shrank in numbers. Some ceased to exist altogether. For, with no valued corporate identity, there was the question; Why stay in a religious community? Why join in the first place? Individual achievement could be just as easily pursued outside. The result was that some for whom the heart of their vocation was a desire for prayer felt called to the hermit life – there was an upsurge in such vocations from the 1960s. Others whose concern was primarily social witness left the religious life to become parish priests, teachers, health or social workers. Those who stayed, and the smaller number who now joined, were left pondering on this issue of identity.

RESISTANCE TO CHANGE

The question then arises as to why many religious communities did not read the 'signs of the time' more quickly and rethink their work and lifestyle sooner. The essential reason is that whatever is deeply ingrained as the basis of 'success' and growth in one era is hard to dislodge in the next, when perhaps a different approach may be more appropriate. This is especially so when the change involves a fundamental shift in identity.

Resistance to change occurred because, first, most communities could not consider abandoning their institutional commitments. The financial viability of some was thought to depend on the institutions they ran. For others, their Rule and charism were linked – inextricably, it seemed to most community members – with these specific works. To abandon them meant the end of the community's corporate vocation. In addition, with fewer vocations, it was harder for members of the order who might want to pioneer something different to be released to do so. They could not be spared, unless the community abandoned its core ministry. The institutions therefore imprisoned many communities, preventing innovation and experiment. The strategy did not save the institutions in the long run: instead the institutions exhausted the community, sometimes to extinction.

Second, the age-profile of most communities had changed by the middle decades of the twentieth century. In the Victorian era, most religious were younger, and with an expanding novitiate drawn from younger people, the average age of members remained low. By the 1950s, many communities had a large group of an older generation, the care of whom occupied a significant amount of the energy of their younger members. In addition, many of the postulants arriving were of more mature age.

Apparent 'growth' in community statistics for the 1950s sometimes hid an ageing membership. A community in 1960 dominated by religious in their fifties had its immediate problems eased by recruiting others of a similar age or a little younger, but in the long run it created an even greater problem of caring for the older generation in the 1970s and 1980s. The older religious also found it difficult to agree to the abandoning of the way of life they had followed for several decades. To be told that a particular practice was no longer required seemed to mock their faithfulness over the years. With fewer younger members, the efforts of many communities to evolve were blocked by sincere but frightened seniors, who held the numerical majority in any vote. It is notable that one of the Anglican communities which embraced change more easily in the 1960s was the Society of St Francis, founded more recently between the world wars. In the mid-1960s, it did not have a single brother over the age of seventy and only a small number in their sixties.

Third, the inherited notion of 'success' requiring visible achievements and increasing numbers hampered any new sense of vision. Often hidden from outsiders, there was a quiet corporate despair at the decline in vocations, which created in turn a lack of confidence. If a tide of new vocations had entered the communities full of new ideas, the leaders might have had the confidence of their Victorian forebears to experiment and launch new initiatives. But in the face of small or empty novitiates, new projects seemed foolhardy. At the same time, changing practices and the internal life of a community would upset the senior generation without necessarily attracting any new vocations. In the wake of their history, it did not seem possible to religious that being fewer in numbers and divesting themselves of their institutions could become an opportunity rather than a defeat. It was not the end of Anglican religious life but only the fading away of a particular expression of it. However, to those facing change, it was hard to embrace such a conclusion.

RENEWING IDENTITY

This essay has suggested that the late twentieth-century crisis of identity for Anglican religious has its roots in history. By understanding the formation of their original identity, Anglican communities can separate the essentials of their charism from those which are bound to an historical context. However, it must be emphasized that the task is not a matter of inventing a 'new' identity. It is about Anglican communities entering deeper into the full tradition of religious life to renew their charism. For Anglican religious life is not a tradition in itself but a part of a movement which has been manifest throughout the centuries of the history of the Church. This means that a Victorian blueprint of community, which grew from particular social and cultural conditions is not the only resource from which Anglican religious can draw. The Victorian founders were choosing aspects of the tradition which suited their particular time and context. Anglican religious today need to do the same.

At the heart of identity, corporate or personal, are relationships, and a particular historical context therefore pushes religious communities into a particular manifestation of their defining relationships: with God, with one another, with the community as a whole, and with the society around them. The pressures arise both from the expectations and criticisms of contemporary society and also from the motivations and perspectives of those called to the life. For example, a society which had created a new and extensive urban poverty in a mere two generations was one in which communities responded with works of mercy and the creation of institutions to expedite their service. A Church which had neglected the Catholic element of its heritage was one in which communities responded by developing a more elaborate spirituality and worship. But these witnesses in themselves were not religious life; they were a particular expression of it.

Throughout the history of Christianity, religious communities have come into being and then disappeared as others have been founded. Those that have survived through different eras have done so either by adapting their identity or by maintaining a broad variety of interpretations of the founder's charism. For example, the Benedictine Rule has been used both by enclosed contemplatives and also by religious running public institutions; and the inspiration of St Francis led to both monastic friars and to brothers wandering from place to place. The essential values of religious life, therefore, have been manifest in diverse ways and adapted to different historical contexts. The mechanism for these changes has been a re-interpretation of the vocation within the four defining relationships which all religious have, mentioned in the previous paragraph.[1] It is the commitment to a deepening of these relationships, not particular works or achievements, which are then the 'call'. It could be suggested that the renewed identity of Anglican religious will not therefore come from finding a 'work' in which to attempt to justify themselves before a predominantly agnostic and secular culture. Instead, it will come in pursuing the Christian life in the set of relationships to which they are called.

1. This fourfold view of the shape of Religious Life has been explored in lectures and other writings of the author, and most particularly in her forthcoming book, *The Drawing of this Love*.

TWO

Change in Anglican Religious Life 1965 – 2000

HILARY OHP

When I joined the Order of the Holy Paraclete in 1960, a few months before the accidental death of our Foundress, Mother Margaret, nothing had changed very much since the Order's foundation in 1915, apart from the fact that it had grown considerably in numbers. I made my life vows in 1963 and then, quite suddenly, everything began to change. Our second Prioress, Mother Anne, encouraged us to respond to the Decree on the Religious Life of the Second Vatican Council (1963-1965) which was mediated to us through the Oxford Conference of Anglican Religious in 1965. It was a 'heady' time to be a young sister, but I would not have missed it for worlds. In this essay, with the help of others, I have looked back over the past forty years and tried to assess the impact of the Vatican Council on Anglican religious life. Finally, I have looked ahead briefly into the new millennium.

In 1955, when Peter Anson wrote *The Call of the Cloister: Religious Communities and Kindred Bodies in the Anglican Communion*, he opened up what was very much a hidden world, little known even to the majority of English churchgoers. The book was well received (it was reprinted in the following year) and must have surprised many of its readers. Anson gave an account of eleven communities for men and sixty for women in Great Britain and Ireland, also another eighteen for men and thirty for women in the rest of the Anglican Church worldwide. Unfortunately, he gave no indication of numbers, but he did show that communities ranged from those with only a single house, to one with twenty branch-houses in England, eight in Africa and three in India. Complete with impressive photographs of their chapels, the book conveys a sense that Anglican communities were as vibrant as they were diverse.

1955 was indeed a high point in the history of most Anglican communities. Novices were flocking in to test their vocations, during the period of idealism after the Second World War. The communities they joined had, for the most part, altered little since their foundation in the years following the revival of Anglican religious life in 1845 – part of the Oxford Movement, which re-emphasised the catholicism of the Church of England. Soon they were all to be challenged, first by the decrees of the Second Vatican Council, which although they carried no authority in the Anglican Church were a considerable influence upon it, and secondly by the social and theological upheaval of the 1960s. All, to a greater or lesser degree, were to undergo changes Anson could never have envisaged as he prepared his book. He was writing, although he did not realise it, at the end of an era.

The Second Vatican Council was also a surprise to all Christians. There had not been a General Council of the Roman Catholic Church since 1869-1870, so no one knew quite what sort of event this was going to be. Pope John XXIII was old and was expected to be a 'caretaker' until his death. Only as the decrees of the Council began to be published did the world realise that nothing short of a revolution was taking place in Rome. There were a few Anglican communities which had close links with their Roman Catholic counterparts either in Great Britain or Europe; for example, the Sisters of Charity, the Poor Clares and the Benedictines of West Malling. They were directly affected by the changes in the Roman Catholic Church which resulted from the decrees of the Council. A few other Anglican communities had begun thinking about change before the Council took place, because there had been a liturgical movement in the Roman Catholic Church which had its effect on some Anglicans too.

For the majority though, the Council only began to impinge when superiors of all Anglican communities received a letter, inviting them to send representatives to a Conference to be held at Christ Church, Oxford, from 28 June to 1 July 1965. The Conference was convened by Dr F. L. Cross, Lady Margaret Professor of Divinity and Canon of

Christ Church, and the Reverend A.M. Allchin of Pusey House, Oxford. Its title was 'The Religious Life in the World of Tomorrow', and its aim was 'to give Religious an opportunity of coming together to study the nature of their vocation, its place in the world and the Church today, and to discuss common problems and interests'. Some 200 Anglican religious attended the Conference from over fifty communities, including some from overseas, and there were a few Roman Catholic observers. Women outnumbered men by two to one, but the six key speakers were all men. Women superiors gave prepared responses after the talks. There were also daily discussion-groups with reporting-back sessions. The Conference was set firmly in the traditional framework of the corporate monastic offices, but 'experimental' Eucharistic Rites from the Church of South India and from the contemplative communities at Fairacres and West Malling were used.

The Oxford Conference of 1965 was not the first time that Anglican religious had met together. There had been a gathering of superiors in Oxford in 1935, which had led to the formation of the Advisory Council on the Relationship of Bishops and Religious Communities. This body, which combines episcopal representatives and religious elected by the communities, has continued to play an important role in the Church of England. In 1969 it was instrumental in setting up the Communities Consultative Council, which soon developed its own important role, as will be explained later. The 1965 Oxford Conference had a wide scope. Not all of the Vatican Council Decree on the Appropriate Renewal of the Religious Life was applicable to the Anglican scene, but the broad principles of the Decree were taken up at the Conference, *i.e.*, the continuous return to the sources of religious life and to the original inspiration behind a given community, and an adjustment of the community to the changed conditions of the times.

One of the main themes considered by the Oxford Conference was contained in the Decree:

There are religious communities which from their rule and institution, combine the apostolic life [i.e. active ministry] with choral office and monastic observance. These should adapt their way of life to the needs of their proper apostolates, at the same time loyally preserving their form of life, for it has been of considerable service to the Church. (n. 9) [1]

Most Anglican communities fell into this category, living what they call the 'mixed life'. Many such communities had been experiencing problems because the demands of professional work, such as nursing or teaching, conflicted with the saying of the monastic Offices at regular intervals during the day. To give one example: in the Order of the Holy Paraclete's branch house at St Hilda's Middle School, after the five resident Sisters had said Sext between the end of morning school and lunch, those teaching in the afternoon went to say None in the sacristy, sometimes leaving one elderly sister to say None at the canonical hour of 3 p.m.

As Anglican communities are autonomous, there was great diversity in their response to the Oxford Conferences of 1965 and to 'follow-up' conferences held in Oxford (1967) and York (1974). A few communities had already been thinking about making changes before the first Conference was held. Some moved rapidly to implement liturgical change while others did it much more slowly. The main overall trend was for the 'mixed' communities to reduce the seven traditional Offices to five or four. Prime was the Office most usually omitted: some also omitted Terce. Sext and None tended to be replaced by a Midday Office. Enclosed communities made less change in this respect: a few who had said the Office in Latin changed to English.

Most communities sooner or later changed the content of the Office. A few adopted the revised Office of the Roman Catholic Church. The Communities Consultative Committee set up by the Advisory Council in 1969 had an Office Book Committee which

---

1. This and all subsequent quotations from the Decree are from *Vatican II: Constitutions, Decrees, Declarations: a new Translation in Inclusive Language*, general editor Austin Flannery, O.P., Dublin, Dominican Publications.

produced an Anglican Office Book adopted by some. There were a few communities who wrote their own revised Office. The general trend was towards simplification: the omission of accretions to the office such as memorials, and an attempt to go behind the medieval to the early form of the Office. The liturgical calendar was also pruned by many communities: feasts of legendary saints were dropped, also most octaves and vigils.

The question has to be asked: did the 'mixed' Anglican communities achieve what they set out to do in this respect? Had they gained a more prayerful liturgy and a more balanced life? Certainly, there was a general feeling that they had achieved a more satisfactory pattern of prayer and work, and it is surely significant that none have gone back to their earlier horarium. However, another problem had begun to raise its head even before the liturgical pattern was changed. Already in the early 1960s, sisters in some communities were taking up full-time employment in the teaching and nursing professions, with some of them as heads of large institutions. This meant that even the revised pattern of the day could create tension between a sister's work and religious duties. Living the 'mixed life' involves coping continually with this kind of tension; and there is no easy way out of it.

The Vatican Decree on the Renewal of the Religious Life had stated as another of its basic principles (n. 2a.): 'Since the ultimate norm of the religious life is the following of Christ as it is put before us in the Gospel, this must be taken by all institutes as the supreme rule'. This signified that the Rule by which each community lived, was to be reviewed in the light of the Gospel. In the 1960s and 1970s most Anglican communities made some revision of their Rule and of their customary (the document which contains the details of their way of life). The influence of Vatican II varied from community to community as did the nature of the changes. A few took a radical line and wrote a new Rule from scratch; others made a piecemeal revision. Some are only now attempting a major rewriting of their Rule.

My own community formed a committee for the revision of the

Rule in 1969, but by the end of 1975, in spite of many meetings, the task had not been completed. It was then decided that three sisters should go to our house at Rievaulx for a week with the commission to write a new Rule. After a few alterations this was accepted by the Order and has been used ever since. The influence of the Vatican Decree on the Church as well as that on the Religious Life is very clear: the Rule contains many references to Scripture, and each of its sections is headed by a biblical quotation. Stress is laid upon the corporate nature of the life, in contrast with the previous emphasis on personal holiness. The vows are seen in a positive light rather than as a means of discipline and self-denial. The entire Rule is centred on Christ. This quotation from the section on celibacy sums up the tenor of the whole:

> Christ is the source of that love which binds us together in the Order, enabling us to love one another fervently with a pure heart and to reach out in universal sympathy and love.

Even if the Rule did not change there were alterations in customs as communities discarded some of their Victorian practices. For example, in women's religious houses, the custom of curtseying to the superior (and even to her chapel stall in her absence) was dropped. More will be said about lifestyle later.

Vatican II made it mandatory for all Roman Catholic religious communities to revise their constitutions (documents describing the ethos and legal requirements pertaining in a particular community) to bring them back to the original spirit of their founders. For a few Anglican communities, this was applicable; but for most, because they had been in existence for a much shorter time than their Roman Catholic counterparts, this aspect of the decree hardly applied. However, some Anglicans did make considerable constitutional changes and have continued to do so. The trend has been towards greater democracy and a less hierarchical style of community government. More recently, communities have had to change their constitutions to comply with charity law in Great Britain.

Another precept of the Decree on Religious Life (n. 2c) was that 'All institutes should share in the life of the Church.' Anglican communities had never seen themselves as apart from the Church, but in many women's communities work had been mainly undertaken in their own schools, homes, retreat houses etc. Influenced partly by the Council, more Anglican women religious began to 'go out to work', usually from a community house. For example, in the 1960s some took up chaplaincy work in universities and hospitals. Since then, as institutional work has gradually been handed over to others, there has been an increase in this move towards pastoral work and spiritual direction, which has brought women religious more into contact with the general life of the Church. After the introduction of synodical government in the Church of England, religious communities began to send their representatives to national, diocesan and deanery synods. More recently, some Anglican women religious have been able to take their place alongside brother religious as deacons and priests. Most communities have networks of oblates or tertiaries who fulfil a double role – supporting the life of the communities by their prayers, and spreading the influence of the religious life far beyond their walls. All this is a far cry from the much more restricted and 'cloistered' existence of Anglican communities before 1960.

One of the areas of renewal which has caused most debate in women's communities has been the religious habit. The Decree on Religious Life (n. 17) was very firm about this.

Religious dress, as a symbol of consecration, must be simple and modest, at once poor and becoming. In addition, it must be in keeping with the requirements of health and be suited to the time and place and to the needs of the apostolate. The dress, of men or of women, which is not in conformity with these norms ought to be changed.

In this area, most Anglican communities have proceeded slowly and few have abandoned the habit altogether. Nevertheless, when compared with pre-1960 styles, all habits show some simplification, and the process of change is not over yet. Some communities now wear the habit only on special occasions, otherwise they wear secular clothes. Many more than in the past have the option of wearing secular dress at certain times, *e.g.*, when on holiday.

This part of the Decree on the Religious Life showed up one of its inherent weaknesses: injunctions were sometimes made by the Council Fathers which were not always backed up by an adequate rationale. Anglican communities have had, therefore, to work out for themselves the arguments for and against the wearing of the religious habit. In the 1970s, the main reason given for wearing the habit was that it was a sign – using the word in the way it was used by the Old Testament prophets. It was thought to convey the message of the Religious Life – total consecration to God – in a way that spoke to people without the need for words. Some Anglican religious still accept this view today. Others now feel that it speaks to people outside the Church of things such as medievalism or sexual repression, which is not what they wish to convey. For some women religious, the veil is seen as a symbol of submission, which, again, is not the message they wish to give to the world. Other women have discarded it for purely practical reasons. These matters will go on being discussed for a long time to come. Meanwhile, the enclosed communities show no signs of discarding the habit, though they have simplified it.

Like the habit, lifestyle in Anglican communities has also changed slowly in the last thirty-five years, probably reflecting social change even more than the direct influence of Vatican II. Diet is one area that has been modernised – suet puddings have given way to salads! There are more informal meals and snacks than in former times. Informality is shown in other ways too: for instance, members of religious communities now generally call each other by their Christian names instead of 'Sister' or 'Brother'. This is also indicative of a greater freedom to make close personal relationships in community. Guests of both sexes are now welcomed more freely into parts of many convents and monasteries. Some communities have been influenced considerably by group dynamics courses, Myers-Briggs workshops, the Enneagram, and the charismatic movement. It could be said that Vatican II introduced the concept of change into the religious life; this in turn has led to types of change which were not conceived of by the Council Fathers!

By the end of the 1970s, the main initial period of change was over, and it is interesting to look back at what Bishop Kenneth Woollcombe said in his Charles Gore Memorial lecture in 1979. Summarising the developments in the years since Vatican II, he was optimistic about Anglican religious life. 'They have entirely revised their liturgy ... revised ... Constitutions to exclude the pettiness of 19th century conventional behaviour ... thought deeply about the theology of the monastic life ... simplified the rhythms of their daily life and their dress ... in short they have effected nothing less than a quiet revolution in the last 20 years.'

The 1985 Advisory Council Report to the House of Bishops on Religious Orders in the Church of England expressed what was probably a more realistic opinion. 'Religious communities have both benefited and suffered, been liberated and diminished by the changes of the past 20 years'.

What was implied by suffering and diminishment in this context? One aspect was undoubtedly the increase in the numbers of religious asking for release and leaving Anglican communities. The report mentions three reasons for this: 'The theological ferment of the past 20 years has been partly responsible. Vatican II, which led to vast changes amongst religious in the Roman Catholic Church, has exerted an influence on Anglicans, though not as much as might have been expected. More significant has been the fact that the whole background of life – social, economic and spiritual – during the 1960s and 1970s called in question life in community as it was then being lived.' Perhaps one should add that some members had been admitted too readily into the religious life without sufficient training and discernment of vocation. It is also true to say that change in any institution always results in some people feeling that their security has been undermined, while others are frustrated because change has not been radical enough. Members of Anglican communities left for both of these reasons, and for many more.

Another cause of suffering in this period was the giving up of long-established institutions. For a variety of reasons, many communities decided to hand over their schools, colleges, hospitals or homes to others. In one case it was the Church of England itself that closed a theological college run by religious. It was not easy for any community to re-establish its identity after its foundation work was gone, not least because of the way the community was viewed by the rest of the Church, though some have done this. Communities which appear to have survived most vigorously were those with a very clear identity which did not depend on 'works' – e.g. the Franciscans, and the enclosed communities – but it is difficult to generalise.

Moving forward to the beginning of the new millennium, the 2000-2001 *Anglican Religious Communities Handbook* estimates that there are about 230 men and 710 women living the religious life in Anglican communities in Great Britain and Europe. (For the whole of the Anglican Communion the figures are 1000 men and 1600 women.) There are far fewer in Great Britain, but far more in the rest of the world than in the 1950s.

How far are the principles of Vatican II still an influence upon them? Perhaps the most influential element has been simply the conciliar principle – the idea of meeting together and sharing. The Communities Consultative Council has arranged national conferences and also regional events from its inception in 1969. Separate conferences have also been held for leaders, novice guardians, junior professed, and novices. These gatherings have been important, not just for the ideas exchanged, but also for the bonds of mutual affection that have grown between religious of different communities. For many years the Communities Consultative Council also produced a periodical, *Encounter and Exchange*, which fostered links between the communities. The conciliar ideal has also flourished within communities, as members are now trained to listen to and learn from one another as well as to God and the Church. It is surely significant that the term 'superior', used for the head of a community, has now largely disappeared. No longer do religious 'sit at the feet of their leader' as they used to do. While still recognising the authority of the one chosen to be in charge, they now value the contribution each member can make to any decision.

Opinions will always differ as to the how important the influence of Vatican II was on the Church of England communities, because as we have seen, they are autonomous and very diverse. Phrases such as 'yeast fermenting' and 'ideas slowly percolating' sum up what has been perceived to have been happening in the forty years since the Council. For most, there is now an acceptance of the fact that change is here to stay. As one religious has said, 'We hope never to stop reappraising, re-evaluating and reflecting on our life and work.' Several communities are at present in the process of making a major revision of their Rule. It appears that the spirit of *aggiornamento* is by no means dead.

However, the fact cannot be ignored that candidates for the religious life in the Church of England are few and far between these days. Viewed from the standpoint of the year 2001, it seems that the Decree did not drive religious deep enough into the essential nature of their vocation. It is always easier to deal with externals than to effect a change of mind and heart: such radical renewal can only come from within, through the promptings of the Holy Spirit. Those young people today who do think deeply are highly critical of anything that does not ring true to what it claims to be. This is a challenge to Anglican religious to go back once again to the ancient inspiration of monasticism and to discern what form it should take in the third millennium. The post-conciliar phase is over: we need a new dynamic for a new era.

Three pointers can be seen as to the way the religious life in the Church of England will probably move in this new century. Having become much closer to the mainstream life of the Church, some religious are now reasserting their belief that in essence their vocation is to be 'on the edge'. The first monks were people who went out into the deserts of Egypt and Syria in the fourth century to find God in solitude and detachment. The hermit life is being lived by a few men and women both in the country places and in inner city areas. This witness to an essential and primitive aspect of monasticism is as much needed in the twenty-first century as in the fourth. Those living in community are also realising that their comfortable lifestyle is in danger of being a betrayal of the call to be counter-cultural and prophetic. We need to ask ourselves, 'What does the vow of poverty mean today?' and 'How do we show its meaning in our everyday lives?'

Another trend is that a few communities have begun to admit people not in religious vows to live alongside them or as part of the group. There is always a tendency for members of religious communities to become hidebound by their rules and constitutions; but now that communities are becoming much smaller it is easier for them to allow for experiments on these lines. Flexibility combined with a firm grasp on the essentials of tradition could make for communities much more attractive to young people today who are looking for an alternative to individualism. There could be a core group in such a community who have made a life commitment but who are totally accepting of others who come for a time and then move on.

Following on from the closer cooperation between communities in the last forty years there are some interesting joint-ventures being undertaken by members of different communities working together. Some are combining for novitiate training courses – particularly valuable when there is only one novice in a community. There are also places where members of two communities work together on a shared project for a certain length of time. For some time now, communities which have only a few members left have combined with another community for their last years. Men and women religious are now involved in joint communities and projects which would have been unthinkable half a century ago.

Lastly, communities are faced with the fact that many young people coming to join them are not 'cradle Christians', which calls for a new approach to the training given in novitiates. It also seems likely, because of trends in the Church, that many in the future will come from an evangelical background rather than from the 'High Church' tradition of the Church of England. Thus, communities are being challenged to look again at what is essential in their lives and what is 'baggage' left over from their past. We are being forced back to the question, 'What is the theological basis of the religious life?' Many of us have long been in the paradoxical state of constantly adapting while remaining basically the same; but the challenges today are very searching indeed. Are we ready to be changed even more radically than we were after Vatican II?

Change can only be in one direction – towards a community life which bears the same stamp as the first Christian community described in the Acts of the Apostles 2:42-47. The Holy Spirit created that community of believers, and is always waiting to do so again if we will allow it to happen. It is God, the Holy Spirit, who is the theological basis of religious life, the only source of Christian community. The Spirit inspired the early monastic leaders and writers, people such as Antony of Egypt, John Cassian and Benedict to create the monastic tradition of liturgy and discipline. Francis and Dominic were inspired to respond to the needs of a different era. In each successive age, the Spirit has re-formed the religious life to supply what was needed at the time. May we be given grace to discern what we should do in this new century.

THREE

Religious Life on the Missions

NICOLAS CR

On a dirt road winding its way up the side of some high African hills an eighteen-year-old student walks with excitement in his heart. The journey from Salisbury,[1] hitchhiking, had been long. At Christmas Pass, before Umtali, there was another long wait before a friendly farmer took him the last ten miles to the St Augustine's turn-off. Now the midday African sun beats down on him as he makes his way up the hill. A car comes past and stops. A delightful black man offers him a lift and engages him in fluent English conversation. This is the first time in all his eighteen years that this white youth has met an African on such equal terms. Not surprisingly, this man, Gilbert Rondizai, is headmaster of the primary school on the mission just ahead.

This was not my first visit to St Augustine's. I had been there just three months before and was captured by the beauty and the spirit of the place. This was 1965. A large brick church with magnificent towers stands on the side of the mountain. Close by it are the buildings of the secondary school, primary school, and teacher training college for which the mission is famous. Below the church are two sets of houses – one the convent of the Order of the Holy Paraclete, the other the convent of the African sisters of Chita cheZita Rinoyera. At the top end of the mission is the oldest set of houses – inhabited by the Fathers of the Community of the Resurrection. There, ten Brethren of the Community live out their busy lives. Some teach in the secondary school. One is head of the teacher training college. Two go out to the district churches – huge areas to north and south with a network of

---

1. In most of this essay I have used the pre-independence names which were in use at the time of its setting.

schools and churches which are supervised from St Augustine's. One is involved in translation work and has a particular ministry hearing confessions. Each morning this group is in church, in their white cassocks and grey scapulars, for Prime and Matins at 6 o'clock. Then Masses are celebrated at altars all round the mission. Breakfast follows in silence, then Terce, and the work of the day begins. For the visitor, the place is quiet and prayerful, and the mountains round about give it a beauty all of its own. At midday, the Community brethren are back for the office of Sext, then lunch. Work follows in the afternoon, punctuated by tea and the little office of None. Evensong at 6.00 is followed by supper, and Compline at 9.00 brings the day to an end. Greater Silence envelopes the priory house, and the young visitor crawls happily into bed, hardly able to believe that such a place exists and that he can be part of it – could even be part of it for always if only they would let him join.

St Augustine's was one of the first missions established in Rhodesia after the arrival of the white people who would rule the country for the next ninety years. Cecil Rhodes gave large tracts of land to certain missions as part of his aim to civilize the new territory named after him. The first Anglican bishop, George Knight Bruce, camped on the new piece of land in 1891. The first work was developed by Douglas Pelly and a series of lay missionaries. In 1902 the Community of the Resurrection arrived in Johannesburg to begin its work in South Africa and in 1915 it was able to take up the invitation to assume responsibility for the work at St Augustine's. The first to arrive were Fr Bertram Barnes, a veteran from the missions in East Africa, who soon became confident in Shona and wrote a useful dictionary of the language, and Fr Robert Baker whose practical work on the mission culminated in the magnificent church building.

St Augustine's was not unique. In many ways it was a classic mission pattern developed by many different denominations in India and throughout Africa. The pattern was that of a strong mission centre with education and health facilities, either because the missionaries wished, through these means, to attract converts, or because they genuinely believed they had a civilizing mission in an uncivilized land. A lot of this health and education work began accidentally. Almost every missionary had a basic knowledge of first aid which produced amazing results in this environment and so the first clinics appeared. A knowledge of reading was necessary for converts to read the Scriptures. Out of this grew the great language work and the schools. Round the mission the new Christians gathered, establishing a kind of safe area where it was easier to maintain their newly acquired faith.

Gradually, mission stations were established at points around the district, each rapidly acquiring a small school, a church, and, perhaps, a resident catechist. At St Augustine's, as with most of the early missions, education included training in industrial skills: tailoring, building, education and carpentry – not usually to a very high level, but enough to make a significant impact on the local economy. In this respect one may see a real parallel between the work of the great mission stations in Africa and the influence that the Benedictines and Cistercians had in Europe during the Middle Ages. In both cases community life gave the strength and resources for a clear living of Christian life which helped to bring the local people into the faith and at the same time gave stability and new expertise to the local economy.

In Zimbabwe there was a number of such Anglican mission stations even before the Second World War – St Faith's Rusape, St Mary's Hunyani, St David's Bonda, All Saints Wreningham, St Patrick's Gwelo, Cyrene Mission in the Matopos. Roman Catholics, Methodists, Dutch Reformed and Baptists had established similar centres. Yet no less a witness than Professor Terence Ranger believes that for a significant number of decades St Augustine's was known throughout the country as the premier centre for African education.[2] It began the first secondary school for Africans in the country, and Herbert Chitepo, the country's first African lawyer and later nation-alist leader, was among its first intake. Amongst Anglicans its influence was incalculable. Boys and girls came from all over the

2. Private conversation, September 2000.

country for education. Many became teachers and, once in their schools, became the catechist leaders of the Christian community there.

What made St Augustine's unique for Anglicans in Zimbabwe was the presence of three religious communities there. All three had a clear monastic identity with an emphasis on worship and the common life. This was not surprising since the Order of the Holy Paraclete had been closely linked with the Community of the Resurrection since its foundation, and together they had evolved a similar understanding of their religious life. Likewise the African sisterhood (CZR) had been founded on the mission by brethren of the Community. Monastic life meant, for all of them, a structured life in which the sevenfold (later the fourfold) office was said faithfully. Silence rules pertained – usually from Compline till after breakfast, and in various places around the convent and priory buildings throughout the day. Yet, at the same time they were engaged in all the multifarious works of running a large mission station and its district churches.

It seemed to work extremely well. The clearly ordered life of a large institution suited the monastic structure of their life. The members of the community (at least the priests) who found such a structure inhibiting, got off into the districts, sometimes for weeks on end. The work was extremely satisfying. African people are particularly responsive to education and there was never any doubt that the work was a success.

Yet beneath this busy, purposeful life there were problems. Within the Community, St Augustine's gained a reputation for being a rather difficult house. Strong characters were sent there to do the work but they found it hard to get on. They tended to immerse themselves in the fascination of teaching, in the administration problems of running a large mission, or in the much more welcoming atmosphere of the outstations. There was little time and energy left over for community life. For the most part, this was simply accepted as part of the way things were. At least three members of the Community of the Resurrection left to become Roman Catholics. One left to get married. It was assumed (perhaps rightly) that these were individual choices not reflecting adversely on the quality of life in the Priory.

In 1951 a crisis of management led the Provincial (Fr Trevor Huddleston) to send Fr Benjamin Baynham from South Africa to be head of the whole establishment. It was an excellent choice in that Fr Baynham was a superb administrator and devoted to the young people on the mission. Those young people, today in late middle age, still recall his memory with deep gratitude and love. But Benjamin was angry at having had to leave work he loved in South Africa and in his seventeen years at Penhalonga never related well to the brethren whose Prior he was. This was a scar which never went away.

Perhaps the most significant area of failure, for the Community of the Resurrection and for almost all religious communities working in Southern Africa (and no part of the Anglican Communion outside England has had so many), was their sheer failure to attract members from the countries in which they worked. In Rhodesia they showed no signs of wanting local people to join.

Numerous reasons were given for this. The commonest was that African people like to marry, and could not accept celibacy. Some Africans who asked to join were told that they could not because they lacked the education or cultural background to be a Community of the Resurrection Father. Rather more Africans of both colours, one suspects, found the sheer Englishness of the religious communities unwelcoming. In the end, two white priests and no Africans found their way into the Community. (In South Africa the story was a little different but not really significantly so.)

Despite their commitment to the people among whom they lived, their own community formed a tightly knit group which meant they could maintain their cultural identity and not merge into the society which surrounded them. Significantly, very few Community of the Resurrection brethren ever gained more than a passing fluency in an African language and most could do little more than struggle through the Mass and sacraments despite years of life amongst African people. Food in the Priory was always very European. Manners were those of the English middle class of mostly public school background. Conversation was light, gossipy and in the English tradition, never very serious. Potentially serious conflicts (such as the political ones arising in the late 1950s and onwards) were carefully avoided, leading to a major breakdown in relationships within the Community during the liberation war.

Added to this was the paternalism inherent in the Community's situation. They were the generous providers. They were also the landlords. They had resources of education, culture, experience which set them apart from the people they worked with. Though not racist in any obvious sense they assumed that it would be a very long time before Africans could genuinely take their place alongside whites. They worked well with Africans themselves but that was different from accepting them as equals in the Community. Africans felt this, and, much as they admired the Fathers, realised they would not easily find a place in this Community.

These are cultural factors, though in fact cultural factors never cease to have an impact on the way religious life is lived, and need to be constantly faced.

One wonders, too, were the brethren failing to live out the religious life? Were they, in fact, no different from other missionaries, except that they wore a distinctive habit and perhaps had a more demanding devotional rule? That may account for the fact that they had no wish to recruit local people into the Community, as they would have done had they been a monastic foundation wanting to establish a monastic community in the country. That might also explain why local people, not particularly wishing to assume the character of foreign missionaries, saw no reason to join these communities, no matter how much they admired them. In this respect they were not unlike the Church Missionary Society in Uganda or the Universities Mission to Central Africa in Tanzania who definitely would not accept local people into their societies because local people could not (in their terms) be missionaries.

The problem, though, is to show in what way they failed (if they did) to live out the religious vocation. They (mostly) kept the Rule. They said their prayers. They worked faithfully at the Community's work. They understood themselves to be religious living under vows and generally valued this identity. When they returned to England they took up life in the Mother House and, though not always without complaint, remained there till the end. To discover failure, if there was one, we need to look to the communities themselves, to the pragmatic, unthoughtful English way in which the religious life was set up and to the on-going reluctance that communities had to alter the relationship of their life and their work.

Anglican religious life sprang into being in the mid-nineteenth century. For a variety of reasons, almost all the women's orders quickly embraced large works which became a real focus of their lives.[3] The first men's communities (those that survived – Society of St John the Evangelist, Society of the Sacred Mission, and Community of the Resurrection) were also quickly heavily committed to work, either of an educational nature, or of peripatetic preaching around the country. It is true that all these communities had, too, a monastic structure and pattern with rules of silence, obedience, corporate prayer and a conscious or unconscious drawing upon the tradition of monastic life as it came to them through some, often unreliable, contemporary sources. For a hundred years or more, the recipe worked very well. Impressive work was done both for the Church and for society. Godly men and women discovered a life of prayer that they would not easily have found elsewhere. A new dimension of Christian life centred on prayer and intercession found its way into the Anglican Church.

Vatican II changed this, or was, at least, the time when all this changed. In common with Roman Catholics in the Western world we found the work we did was no longer necessary, or no longer compatible with religious life. Institutions came under attack in the 1960s. A life of such structured inflexibility seemed incompatible

3. See Susan Munn's *Stolen Daughters, Virgin Mothers* (Leicester University Press, Leicester, 1999) for a fascinating account of this.

with the life of a Pilgrim Church living the simplicity of the Gospel. Schools which had pioneered women's education, or had simply served the poor had now become fee-paying schools for the better-off. Children's homes and other kinds of social work had been taken over by the State.

However, most of these communities had attracted people whose motive for joining was at least influenced by the work the Community did. In this they found a fulfilment and an identity which they could value and other Christians could understand. So the search began for other kinds of work, for work that took place in society, for work done from small houses, or for work that would still fill the large houses we had inherited. In Africa, the schools were handed over to the Church, the convent and priory buildings became teachers' houses. The mission work was given to local priests and in a surprisingly short time the great communities have shrunk to a remnant of elderly brothers or sisters, still working hard, still happy in their work, and loved by others. Yet few local people are drawn to join them in their religious life. Something is missing, some vision, perhaps, has departed.

One of the problems in all this, in both England and Africa, may have been the manner in which authority came to be exercised. When religious orders ran many public works, religious were people of real influence and power. Sisters and Brothers found themselves in charge of enterprises which affected the lives of hundreds. Theirs was the responsibility to run them efficiently, to make best use of scant resources, to encourage, teach and, from time to time, discipline their charges. This was inevitable with the nature of their work and it was mostly well done. Yet the image of the Beatitudes, which some would place at the heart of the religious life, was often far from them. Simply to be a figure of great authority in an establishment seemed to contradict the following of a Christ who came 'not to be served but to serve' (Mk 10:45). The conflict was heightened when the differences between the religious in charge of the mission departments and the people who worked for them were highlighted by skin colour. This introduced a new and complex ingredient into the relationship between missionaries and the people of Africa. For the most part, at least in Zimbabwe, it is clear that missionaries of all denominations were greatly loved and appreciated. Inevitably, there were conflicts on missions when tenant farmers stepped out of line; when Christian employees took second wives, when white missionaries agreed too obviously with the racist attitudes of other white people. Yet when the political consciousness of the 1960s and 1970s began to heat up, missionaries on the whole were excepted from the criticism of whites. (On the other hand, missionaries were seen by most white people as dangerous agents of sedition and a source of corruption to the innocent native!) In the rhetoric of African nationalism some criticisms were made of the Church and its missionaries for helping the white government to steal the land from black people. Schools, from time to time, experienced political riots which could seem to be directed at the white teachers and priests, but could be more accurately understood as an expression of frustration with the whole governing order.

When civil war came to Zimbabwe it was not often directed against the Churches. Several missions did close; several white missionaries (and far more black Christian leaders) were killed. The reasons were sometimes political, sometimes personal, but never seemed to be part of a general anti-mission ideology, more the accident of war. St Augustine's was one of the few mission-stations where white priests remained throughout the civil war. In some ways, that was a witness to the strength of Community life which gave the brethren greater courage and security. It also testified to the support which the local people gave to the Community. Had they given bad reports to the local guerrillas, the priests would certainly have had to leave. This never happened and the Prior, Fr Keble Prosser, worked quite well with the local guerrilla leader. In fairness to other missions which did close, one should add that St Augustine's was only a few miles from Umtali, and though dangerous, particularly at night, was far less so than most other mission stations further out in the countryside.

The Order of the Holy Paraclete sisters withdrew from St Augustine's in 1978. In 1983, after a considerable amount of wrangling both in the Community and outside, the Community of the Resurrection withdrew from St Augustine's, handing over responsibility for it to the diocese of Manicaland, though with Fr Prosser still the Principal. The reasons for leaving were many. Numbers within the Community of the Resurrection were no longer sufficient to sustain such a work, and the newer members of the Community had no desire or aptitude for that kind of missionary work. Black Zimbabweans were now well able to run such a school themselves, and most of the outstations were now independent districts under Zimbabwean priests. Within the Community, there was a clear perception that this kind of work was no longer appropriate to the religious life. Unhappily there was no agreement as to what was appropriate; so, no new work or manner of living came out of this withdrawal.

Amongst Zimbabweans there was much disagreement too. Some were glad to have the school fully in the diocese. Many, however, felt betrayed and abandoned by the Fathers and, nearly twenty years later, still feel the Community should have stayed. This is not because the work collapsed without them. The school itself continues to excel and regularly produces the best A-level results in the country. The mission work has been much more problematic and haphazard in its performance.

Yet even among those who so strongly believe the Community of the Resurrection should have stayed, there are criticisms. The chief of these was that the Community of the Resurrection, like the Anglican Church generally in Rhodesia, did little to prepare real leaders amongst African people. Good parish priests there were, but none was sent overseas for wider experience or theological training until just before the first was consecrated as a bishop. Many teachers there were, but mostly in primary schools. They were not encouraged to press ahead with further study, and those who did worked on their own. When the time came to appoint African headmasters of secondary schools, very few Anglicans could be found. There is no doubt that leadership in all areas of Anglican Church life in Zimbabwe since 1980 has been poor and uninspired. The Community of the Resurrection must share in the lack of imaginative training which led to this.

Another criticism offered by those who worked at St Augustine's was the fact that the Community Chapter decided everything. All decisions about the school and the out-stations went through the Chapter (that is, the Community of the Resurrection brethren alone). The teachers had little say, except those, like the few longstanding white teachers who were friendly with the brethren. In one sense this was natural since all finance came through the Community, but it failed to respect those with whom brethren worked, and did not see them as more than employees or not quite grown-up children. Sadly, this kind of paternalist and disrespecting attitude has not been limited to Africa.

That brings us to the final point of this essay. St Augustine's Priory was a particular case which felt itself (and was often perceived to be) very different from the other houses of the Community, especially in England. One could then see the problems and failures of the Community there, as well as its successes, as a closed chapter of purely historical interest. This would be a short-sighted failure to use the experience of this Priory to understand elements of Anglican religious life which need to be recognised if the religious life is to develop into the future. The failure to resolve the question as to whether the community was essentially missionary or monastic made it difficult to adapt to a new self-understanding in Southern Africa when this particular phase of work came to an end. In both South Africa and Zimbabwe, work which the Community had done for decades and with which it had identified itself came to a right and proper end. The attitude of a majority then was that it was simply time to leave the work to others and go. A small minority looked around for other similar work. Another minority asked whether it was not part of our monastic vocation to attempt to plant the religious life, in the Community of the Resurrection's particular form, in the new African societies emerging. This question made no sense to the majority who saw the Community's vocation simply to do a particular missionary or educational job. The work could now be left to others and the remnant could return to retirement in England.

A second aspect of the Community of the Resurrection which, to some extent, has been true of most of the men's communities (and some of the women's) in the Church of England has been its background in the English public schools and the colleges of Oxford and Cambridge. In many ways, this has been a great strength since the Oxbridge colleges in a real way preserved the traditions of their monastic or religious foundation before the Reformation and passed this on to the Community in the tradition of common worship, common life and sound learning. Likewise, the experience which the majority of early brethren had in public schools gave them invaluable experience in living closely together, in accepting discomfort and the curtailing of personal freedom in the greater freedom of answering the Community's call

However, public schools also teach boys that survival depends often on maintaining an act, on not revealing emotions, on not talking about the deeply personal. The Community of the Resurrection, at least, has tended to maintain a level of courtesy and good behaviour which has often prevented real communication, especially when difficulties emerged in an individual's life. This led many to real isolation within the Community and a consequent need to find their human needs fulfilled outside it. More seriously the conventions of what was the proper way of living together often overrode the commands of the Gospel. The weakness, penitence and forgiveness which make the Gospel so difficult to live in the Western world did not always find a more ready home in the Priory than it found in the world at large.

A third failure lies in the tendency of any institution to lose its flexibility and cease to change. The Community at St Augustine's failed to see the way in which various paternalist responses to the African people, particularly within the local Church, were no longer appropriate. More imaginative thinking would have enabled them to take a more adventurous part in preparing the Church for an independent Zimbabwe. A more serious application to their missionary responsibility would have made more of them fluent in Shona and properly conversant with Shona culture. In fact, they remained the typically good-hearted English amateurs, so making themselves irrelevant when the situation demanded real knowledge in these areas.

Likewise, the failure to recognise that working with other people must be done on a real basis of equality and respect in the end made the Community's control of its life and work a negative factor in its ability to respond to the new Zimbabwe in a way which may have given it a future there. Sadly, this pattern has repeated itself in England, in the Community of the Resurrection and elsewhere, and the warnings given by the withdrawal or disappearance of most of the communities who worked in Southern Africa are not attended to.

Were the seventy years the Community of the Resurrection spent in Zimbabwe a failure, then? In no terms can they be understood as such. As a work of primary evangelism, the Community established a large area of very enthusiastic Anglican Christians with churches, priests, schools and a glorious tradition of which they are very proud. As a work of education, at least in terms of the primary schools which provide education to thousands of children, and the secondary school which continues to impart the highest standards of appropriate learning, there is a great deal to be proud of. It could be argued that in its latter years the Community became so focussed on maintaining its works that the institutional tendencies of Catholic Christianity came to dominate and the kind of religion practised lacked (and continues to lack) the heart which makes Christian life so compelling and life-changing. That would be a question this essay cannot discuss.

In the end, however, the Community did not establish itself in Zimbabwe in a form that made it possible for Zimbabweans themselves to become a part. For most in the Community, that is not a failure since it was never the intention of the Community to do so. For those of us who believe Zimbabwe needs a form of the monastic life which can offer the monastic vocation in terms which are appropriate to the changing African world, that failure is a serious one which needs to be accepted and thought through for the sake of the Community's future, even in England.

Although the Community of the Resurrection has long since gone from St Augustine's, happily the story is not yet ended. Within the diocese there remains great affection and a real sense of calling amongst many former pupils to re-establish the vision of a mission establishment with a ministry beyond that of the fine secondary school. It would be encouraging to see this as more than education and development work and something a lot closer to the loving service of God which inspired the first Brethren to join the Community of the Resurrection and come to Africa.

This may be found in another tangential off-shoot. In Gokwe in the north west of the country a remarkable priest has founded a community of friars and sisters which is flourishing. Fr Lazarus Muyambi, himself married, seems to have taken on the role of a Carter or Butler in bringing together young men and women into the Chita cheZvipo zveMoto. This community bears remarkable similarities to the Community of the Resurrection and the Order of the Holy Paraclete. The members are devout, hard-working and increasingly well-trained in teaching, nursing and other skills valuable to the work of development. One is only tempted to ask again – are they religious, or primarily Church workers? Is there a difference? Can they be helped to avoid the temptations into which an earlier generation fell?

FOUR

Religious Life 'On the Streets'

SISTER ANNALIESE CSC

'THE SABBATH WAS MADE FOR HUMANKIND' (Mk 2:27)

It is the middle of Sunday afternoon, and the usual weekly 'street party' is taking place in our yard. In the space of two hours we expect between 200 and 270 visitors who come for a food parcel and a chat. Twelve volunteers are well occupied, some in serving drinks, and cakes donated from local bakers, while others are busy giving out carrier bags of tins and cereal. For those who come early, there is also bread, tea-bags and pasta, but only at Harvest and Christmas is there enough of those to go round. People soon gather around the flowers by the notice I have put up to 'see who it is this time'. Sandy died in the week, of septicaemia. She was just thirty-five.

I am a member of a religious order, the Community of the Sisters of the Church, that has, from its foundation in 1870, sought to combine a life of adoration and active service. Our Mother Founder, Emily Ayckbowm, placed us under the patronage of St Michael and the angels. We read in Scripture that the angels 'stand in the presence of God', while at the same time serving God as messengers of divine love and care (Lk 1:19). While we can never attain the angelic heights, we can let their twofold vocation be a living inspiration for us.

Sister Rosina and I are on our usual 'playground duty' amidst the crowd, with dogs and children forever under our feet . Belinda arrives with another black eye. She doesn't want to talk about it. A pensioner called Clive, comes up to tell me the latest about his wife who is severely disabled after a car accident. He cares for her faithfully. 'If she dies,' he says, 'I'll just lay down beside her and die too. I've been saving up my pills.' I can only touch his hand and assure him of my love and prayers.

The 'pram brigade' arrive from a local Social Services parent-and-baby home: I go to greet the young mums and of course admire their offspring. They are all delighted with the selection of baby clothes we have had from some local Churches. 'Mr Steak and Kidney' sweeps in on his bike with his usual request for a meat pie, while three people empty the contents of their bags of tins near my feet and begin a 'swap shop'. Someone tells me that Lorna is back in hospital. One of the many ulcers on her leg has burst and she can barely walk. I find myself wondering if she will ever see her fortieth birthday.

While all this is going on a commotion seems to be taking place at the open window where Jean is serving the refreshments. I go to see what is going on to find the same young man has pinched the sugar bowl for the second time in the afternoon (there are other white powders even more sought after on our streets but sugar is still the source of many arguments in our yard). Jean decides to put the sugar in the drinks directly while the culprit makes himself scarce, only to return, repentant, later in the afternoon with a bunch of stolen flowers which we put into chapel.

'STAY WITH US, BECAUSE IT IS ALMOST EVENING
AND THE DAY IS NOW NEARLY OVER' (Lk 24:29)

Any reference to Sunday as the Sabbath day of rest always gives rise to more than a few laughs in our house. It is 5.30 p.m. and now, having preached at church, fed twelve for Sunday lunch, and supervised the distribution of over 250 food parcels during the afternoon, I am on the phone placing the order in for another van-load of 1,400 tins tomorrow. Then we will say Evensong.

We have had a Community house here in Bristol for nearly ten years now. We came in response to an invitation from the Bishop and the then Rector of our parish to be a praying community in the heart of the city and to be open to respond to the needs around us. Inevitably, there has been no shortage of needs to respond to! However, as well as living together, praying and seeking to help those who come to us in need, we are also members of our local community of St Paul's which is a colourful area – full of vibrant and warm-hearted people. When the house was set up, we were four sisters (of around 28 in this country) and over the recent years we have been just three, or two sisters and a resident volunteer. In Community life we are always 'more than the sum of our parts' and here in Bristol, we draw support not only from our wider Community of Sisters but also our local parish church St Agnes, parishes throughout and beyond the city, and a wide circle of associates and friends. We know these relationships to be mutually enriching,

Our food parcel ministry – the aptly named 'Five Loaves and Two Fishes' project – exists entirely through the generosity of around fifty different parishes (and some individuals) who collect food and money for us regularly. We could not manage such an apparently crazy scheme without them or without our wonderful team of over thirty-five volunteers . We also have three unemployed men who work with us voluntarily almost full time – helping with all the heavy deliveries as well as answering the door.

I certainly didn't enter the religious life to manage a free food service, it just seemed to grow out of our life here. But when we do join the religious life, we need (as Judith, our former superior told me) to put all ideas of ourselves on a long piece of elastic! With our availability we offer to God and our community, our potential, the blank cheque of ourselves, along with our willingness and readiness to be surprised!

For me, the religious life is firstly about union with the Beloved, and it is only immersed in Christ that I can seek to offer a presence of love to those who come to our door. Our Community Rule of Life says: 'To learn to pray well, we need to pray much.' In this inner city house we begin our day with an hour of personal quiet and meditation before meeting together for Morning Prayer. It is in that hour with the One who 'has made me his own' (Phil 3:12c) that I am renewed and resourced for the day (even though I might not always be aware of this at a feeling level). As a religious, I believe that we too must be challenged to face our own frailties and need, to know ourselves known and accepted absolutely where we are most vulnerable and wounded . We are invited to say and become 'yes' to the One who says and is 'yes' for each us, and to drink daily from the cup of unending and unconditional love offered to us. And although our reaching out can never fully mirror the perfect love with which we are loved, with grace, water can be turned into wine and our ministry can be a vehicle of the touch of God.

It is not, then, about givers and receivers, or about those who have much and those who have little. It is about being alongside one another, sharing the burdens, the struggles and the joys and fun of life. And here, living surrounded by far more suffering than we can ever respond to, we must also be able to take care of ourselves, be prepared to take risks, make mistakes and forgive ourselves and one another. Even though we live and breathe an air where evil is often quite tangible, we must not forget to enjoy the gift of life – go for a swim, visit friends, go to the pictures, and have fun outside the endless need that could threaten to swallow us up.

Anyone who has lived in community will know that it is not an easy option – living closely (with people one didn't chose) especially in a small group, one is inevitably confronted with one's own weaknesses and limitations as well as those of other community members! It takes a large dose of humour, generosity of heart and openness to the constant stirrings of the Spirit to find the courage to begin each day anew, believing in each other and the life to which we are called.

The added pressure of living in an area renowned for drug-dealing and with all the associated problems of addiction, violence, crime and prostitution can take its toll. Many of the people who come to our house feel that they have few or no choices in their lives – some seem to spiral ever deeper into chaos. In order to be as available as possible, and to guard our own inner well-being, we need to be aware how easy it is to absorb feelings such as powerlessness, desperation, or rage, and that at times it may be helpful to share these feelings with each other, with a supervisor or with a friend.

Being in daily contact with some of the most marginalised people in our society means being in touch with life 'on the edge', where the next 'fix', the next meal, and the next place to lay down one's head (usually in that order) are often the most predominant concerns. The poor of our society can teach us a lot about living in the present moment. Many of them have very little else.

Life on the edge is characterised by instability on nearly all levels. Most of the women I meet who work in prostitution, for instance, were abused as children and are now with an abusive partner or pimp. It would be foolish to think that our long-term presence here can reach into the depth of such wounds, but we can perhaps offer them something that is for them 'counter-cultural', perhaps even a holding-place or a brief resting-place.

There is absolutely nothing romantic about being poor. Christ came to call all of us to fullness of life. As Christians, we are responsible to care for those who do not even have the basic necessities of life. We must never be satisfied with providing handouts but be ever ready, in whatever way we can, to be a voice for the voiceless.

'AT THE FOOT OF THE CROSS ... ' (Jn 19:25)

It is Good Friday: in St Paul's, our carnival-like ecumenical 'procession of witness' reaches a local Green. The Salvation Army plays away lustily while friends chat and greet each other in the sunshine. A few serious souls armed with leaflets look around fervently for customers to be saved!

A young woman I know well from a local hostel comes up to me clearly distressed. She is being threatened and pleads with me for some money to pay off a small debt. It is a hard day to be firm about such things; so I break all my own rules and promise to give her something when the procession is over. Having been lured by an enchanting and enormous dog, we find ourselves standing together under the life-sized cross which is now standing upright while the faithful listen to a testimony and call to more faith. My young friend snuggles up to me needing reassurance and then, during the prayers, she looks up at the cross and asks me, ' Is that like the one which Jesus died on?' I said, 'Yes, it is'. Satisfied with the answer, she withdraws her barely concealed bottle of cider to take a long comforting drink.

Later on, after the procession, I gave her the money, two tins of rice pudding (her favourite brand) and a bag of little Easter eggs. She looked at me and said, 'Some people are meant to be here on earth, those like you who help others. I'm not even meant to be here.' Nothing I said could convince her otherwise.

'I HAVE CALLED YOU FRIENDS' (Jn 15:15)

Bert's wife, Annie had died yesterday. I sit in the scruffy smoke-filled room amidst the beer-cans and the despair. Bert, barely articulate through drink and grief muttered, 'Forty years wasted, nothing left.' With him sat his grown-up daughter and the son who was still on speaking terms with him, trying to begin the funeral arrangements. Together with them are his two friends, showing me what friendship is really about. Gus, a huge guy perched on a ridiculous stool (in order to give me a chair) with his tiny dog close by, neither spoke or moved, while Fred helped to search for some missing papers. Because there was nothing that he could say or do, Gus said nothing and did nothing, but he was there and his whole being was holding the unbearable pain of the situation. In him that day I saw Christ.

'HE WAS GREATLY DISTURBED IN SPIRIT AND DEEPLY MOVED' (Jn 11:33b)

It was evening on the day of Annie's funeral. Gus, Fred and dog stood at the door, drenched with rain and grief. They had come to say thank you for the lift I had given them to Annie's burial and to apologise for their friend who had thrown up in the back of the car. Gus had been 'dry' for eight months, but Annie's death was too much and he had needed a few cans to cope. 'She was like a mother to me,' he said. After an inept attempt to dry them off by the gas fire I took the three of them into Chapel to offer warmth to their hearts and souls. 'This is a place of peace,' said Gus, and knelt straight down on the floor, reverently making the sign of the cross. Faithful, smelly, wet dog stayed close by, while Fred lit a candle.

'IN THE IMAGE OF GOD

THEY WERE CREATED' (Gen 1:27, paraphrase)

A typical weekday afternoon in our house: our faithful men volunteers are unpacking some deliveries with the shopping trolley which one of our customers 'acquired' for us from a local super store (I reckon it to be part of their charitable giving which they know nothing about!). In between they are also helping to serve food parcels while our 'regulars' have been invited in as always. Arthur arrives first, a frail older gentleman, only sober when broke, and who, despite limited eyesight, maintains a mischievous twinkle in his eyes. He sits down on our sofa inquiring if we have anything stronger than tea or coffee on offer and having no success on that score, checks out whether there is anyone around today who might like to marry him!

Gertie, who has considerable mental health needs, has brought her usual lengthy shopping list and wanders around clutching Ethel (a large stuffed ape we keep for such purposes). Gertie reports that the teddy bear we gave her (which she has named after me!) has now had a hysterectomy 'to prevent her having babies all over the place'. I refrain from asking whether the said bear was given an anaesthetic for such major surgery!

Karen, a quiet young woman who used to work on the streets, sits and drinks her tea. As always she will only take three or four tins and some biscuits in her concern that there be enough to go round. Like Gertie, Karen has no cooking facilities, only a kettle, and so the choice we can offer is limited.

At this point, Angelina calls in. Angelina is convinced that the whole world is involved in some complex plot against her. She collects detailed evidence of the movements of the most prominent suspects and carries the evidence with her at all times. She comes most days – sometimes five times in one day, though we discourage long visits more than twice a week. While it is clear to her that we too are all part of this conspiracy, she knows that nobody else will listen to her angry accusations and dry her tears. Sister Rosie takes her into our quiet room, but Angelina's shouting is hard to ignore.

One of our Irish mothers, Maria, calls with a trail of children. While one of our volunteers begins to get some food for her, I go and find a jar of lollipops. We have about six Irish women who come, all needing sizable food parcels, each having between six and eight offspring. At Christmas time the number increases considerably as word spreads around the Irish community that the Anglican nuns have a supply of children's gifts! Rosie has helped Maria apply for a grant for a washing machine and she is delighted that the application has been successful.

At this point Karen leaves, promising to return in a few minutes with her pet rat to show us. Gertie, not at all impressed at this proposal, gathers her things and disappears hastily! Once the Irish family has left I take the opportunity to have a mug of tea myself and take it out in the garden to join Arthur who has gone to have a smoke. Pleased to have me to himself for a few moments Arthur invites me again to go around to bless his new flat and, then, adds with glee, 'Stay on and make mad passionate love!'

'BLESSED ARE THE POOR IN SPIRIT' (Mt 5:3)

Sitting in my room after Evensong, relishing some quiet before supper and before I go out on the van, I am suddenly aware of the sound of breaking glass. Because we've had our windows smashed in twice in so many weeks I hurry downstairs to investigate, I find Sister Rosina in the corridor listening to Angelina's latest drama. Rosie and I are more cautious but Angelina insists we go out immediately to see what has happened. We quickly find a rather pathetic looking character standing by our dustbins who points out in a helpful manner the window he has just broken! He had come for some food while we were in Evensong and, having got no response, was registering his protest. It would seem that his previous recent 'protests' at 4 a.m. and 11 p.m. were for the same reason. While Rosie went to phone the police I made some feeble attempts at reasoning with our caller who asked if I minded if he smoked while we waited for the police to arrive. I found myself feeling exasperated and rather sorry for this bedraggled man whose fixation with our windows was so obviously a cry for help. I tried to give some friendly advice, 'Try a change of career – you're not making a good go of this one.' He agreed!

When three police officers arrived, my heart sank as I watched him put his hands out meekly for the handcuffs. The only picture in my mind's eye was of Judas handing over Jesus.

'JESUS SAID: "I AM THIRSTY".' (JN 19:28)

Since its founding in 1995 1 have been part of the *One25 Project,* a registered charity working with women involved in prostitution in our area. From very humble beginnings we now have a drop-in centre open five afternoons a week, employ seven staff, have fifty volunteers, and run an outreach programme four nights a week in a bright yellow van. I go out one night most weeks on the van where we welcome anything from fifteen to over forty, of the hundred or so women who work in prostitution on our streets. In these women I meet Jesus, Jesus who is beautiful but broken, Jesus who is reaching out and dependent on our response.

The following poems are extracts from my journal written on two separate occasions on winter evenings. I did not intend to share them further but have come to realise that they may give a real glimpse into the reality of life on the streets.

You showed me the bruises
beneath your simple clothes,
the strangle marks on your neck
and the wounds of your heart.
You shared the desperate violent attempt
to *kill the memory*
and bleach your body clean
in your inability to grasp
that it wasn't your fault.

I wanted to lash out in hatred and rage,
but where? at whom?
at what human monster?
I don't even want to believe that anyone is capable
of such hideous violation of a life.
I just don't understand –
before what evil am I standing?
You chose to sell sex – but that which you sell
was brutally taken from you
while you lay beaten unconscious,
and left like litter on the street
where the air is heavy with shame.

I feel you showed me a horror no film could ever create –
and yet you kept smiling,
and perhaps more than anything
it was your smile that broke my heart.
I kept trying to reach you with all my strength,
wanting you to hear
that you are a lovely young girl
and that what you have suffered is appalling,
no words are adequate …
It is *not* your fault –

but I am unsure if you can hear anything,

and the air remains heavy with
lies, deceit, greed, violence
and evil.

And my words are drowned by your experience.

I touch your bruises gently – for perhaps a touch can say more,

and you leave; still smiling.

The Beloved comes to me in the stillness
and passes me the Chalice of the bitterness and the sweetness
and the fullness of life;
and I drink and drink,
and I look into the wild eyes of a young girl –
frantic for her next fix, unsure if she will hit me in her frenzy;
silently I wish her peace
and she disappears as quickly as she came
while another girl remarks casually, *she'll be the next one dead.*
And I drink and drink
and I hold the frozen hand of a young girl no longer able to feel the
        cold
and no longer able to give her children a home,
I drink and drink massaging the hands
that remain stubbornly as frozen as ice.

I drink and words choke in my throat
as a stunningly beautiful girl clutching the hot water bottle
kindly advises another
on the gruesome details of injecting when most veins are de-
        stroyed.
Powerless and sick inside I pass them
coffee and egg sandwiches, sponge cake and condoms.

I've had enough now
but you hand me again the cup I cannot refuse,
I drink
and listen to the horrific tale
of another girl calmly recounting the details of a recent attack–
her bruised face a small sign of the brutality
which left her alone and unconscious on a freezing cold night
in a dark street.
She hasn't eaten for two days
and with strange dignity munches her sandwiches slowly
while telling us that she has worked on the streets

since she was 13 and is sure that God takes care of her.

But where were you? I cry out
to the one who passes me the Cup of Life
and there is no answer.
I drink in silence.

A young woman hugs and kisses me warmly –
she dreams of being free of drugs
and getting her children back out of care.
I encourage and challenge her
and wish her well as she disappears into the dark unfriendly night.
I drink again,
and welcome them one after the other,
so many beautiful lives battered and broken, used and abused,
and I look into weary eyes, angry eyes, fearful eyes, desperate eyes.
And I pass around hot chocolate and bananas,
chocolate and crisps and warn them of the latest *Ugly Mug*.
We laugh together as they complain about the police
and then they leave – one after the other
(not without my silent blessing)
and go back onto the streets
and I go home to a warm bed.

The Beloved takes me into his arms again
but I am angry now
and beat his chest with my fists and he doesn't resist
which is unbearable,
so my protests quickly turn into tears
which mingle with yours – indistinguishable
water and wine
who else? you say
will weep for them with me?

FIVE

Transforming Missionaries: The Melanesian Brotherhood

BROTHER RICHARD MBH

In the centre of the City of Chester, in June 2000, a member of the Melanesian Brotherhood, in his black uniform and white sash, was asked by a passer-by. 'What are you doing in the UK? Are you a sports club or music group?' 'No,' he replied, 'I am a missionary.' There was awkward silence, for the word 'missionary' for many carries a lot of negative associations: indoctrination, exploitation, moral condemnation, the destruction of indigenous cultures, the forceful sale of European civilizations, men and women who crossed continents in the name of God but who left behind the very conditions in which material interest would flourish. And today new associations of door to door evangelists disturbing us with what seem like fanatical or miserable creeds praying on the vulnerable. Where did this young black Melanesian fit into this whole picture? 'You're a missionary? I suppose we need missionaries too these days,' the questioner said and laughed, as if nothing could be more absurd.

Yet is it absurd? Or is it possible that never before has the Church needed missionaries so much? If this is to be the case we need to discover not only how mission can transform but how mission must transform the missionary. Can these Melanesian missionaries help us to see again what it means to be a follower of Christ?

In the South Pacific, to the north east of Australia, Melanesia stretches in an arc of islands from Papua New Guinea, through the Solomon Islands, to Vanuatu. Initial missionary work began here in 1847 when Bishop George Augustus Selwyn, first Bishop of New Zealand, made his first voyage of exploration and founded the diocese of Melanesia in 1861. The Church of Melanesia, as it is now known, covers both Solomon Islands and Vanuatu, and was inaugurated as an independent province in the Anglican Communion in 1975. It now has more than 120,000 members and seven dioceses.

One of the unique aspects of the Anglican Church in this Province has been the rapid growth of religious life. There are four religious orders in the Solomon Islands today: the Melanesian Brotherhood, the Sisters of Melanesia, the Society of St Francis, and the Sisters of the Church. The first two of these communities are indigenous to Melanesia and were founded by Melanesians. Judging by vocations and influence, religious life is continuing to flourish and grow at a time when within the rest of the Anglican Communion there has been a decline in vocations. One of those orders, the Melanesian Brotherhood, has now become the largest male religious order in the Anglican Communion. For the last ten years I have worked closely with this community, first as a tutor, then as their chaplain, and now as a brother myself. In this essay I would like to look at the missionary spirit which influenced this community's formation and growth, its methods and spirituality and to look at the potential of such a community for mission within the wider Church.

BISHOP GEORGE AUGUSTUS SELWYN

Bishop George Augustus Selwyn who became the first Bishop of New Zealand in 1841, and who pioneered the Melanesian Mission, became a role model for mission in the Pacific, which was more than simply accommodation: it was based on what he called an 'episcopate of love'. He made two rules for his time in these Pacific islands. Firstly, he would never go where Christians were already at work; he did not want a divided Christianity:

> I can speak from observation, ranging from nearly half the Southern Pacific Ocean, that wherever this law of religious unity is adopted, there the gospel has its full and unchecked power.[1]

He had an unwritten agreement with the London Missionary Society

1. Robert Atwell, *Celebrating the Saints*, Canterbury Press, Norwich, 1988.

and the Presbyterians in the New Hebrides not to invade each other's spheres of work, and this agreement has been observed ever since.[2]

Secondly, Bishop Selwyn believed that the mission should never try to make converts observe English customs and ways of life. He wanted their Christian faith to be 'clothed in Melanesian forms'. His conception was for a new form of missionary outreach which would not rely on resident European missionaries but would work through a Melanesian 'Native Ministry ... Melanesian teachers would Christianize their own communities from within.'[3] He believed that Melanesians would become effective teachers for their own islands and that ultimately there would arise a Melanesian Church free from foreign oversight, free to evolve its own forms of worship and discipline.[4] In his faith in Melanesians themselves, their intellectual powers and moral earnestness, he was about eighty years ahead of the Roman Catholic Church in the Solomon Islands.[5]

JOHN COLERIDGE PATTESON

While many criticised the practicality of Selwyn's vision and saw his restless missionary spirit more as an attempt to ignore his administrative responsibilities in New Zealand,[6] nevertheless this vision never left the Melanesian Mission and was taken up by his protege John Coleridge Patteson, an Englishmen, who became the first Bishop of Melanesia in 1861 . He is still remembered with love and reverence by the whole Church of Melanesia.

What was remarkable about his ministry was the quality of his love for the people of Melanesia and the genuine trust and respect he gave

2. Charles Fox, *Lord of the Southern Isles*, Mowbray, London, 1958, p. 6.
3. H. W. Tucker, *Memoir of the Life and Episcopate of George Augustus Selwyn*, London, vol. I p. 250.
4. David Hilliard, *God's Gentlemen: a History of the Melanesian Mission*, University of Queensland Press, 1978, p. 10.
5. The possibility of developing indigenous clergy in the Solomon Islands was not seriously voiced by the Marist missionaries until 1939. Bishop Boch had stated in 1928 that Melanesians simply lacked the intelligence for priesthood although he said he was satisfied with their "unquestioning if uncomprehending belief" (*Catholic Missions in the Solomon Islands*, p. 147)
6. Hilliard, op. cit., p. 13.

to them: he developed a relationship with the indigenous people that challenged the whole foundation of colonial prejudice. The Victorian Anglican Church of this time still believed very much in the English way of doing things, an attitude summed up by Bishop Tait of London: 'the more they remain like ourselves the better.' [7] This was the time when much mission literature was characterising the heathen as primitive, superstitious, dishonest, dangerous, savage and dirty.[8]

Patteson comes from the Victorian Church and his own attitudes are obviously the result of his upbringing. For example, writing to his uncle in 1856, he talks about the need for an improved style of native house and greater cleanliness when eating the food; but, because of his commitment to the people, we find him in this same letter breaking through cultural prejudices and reaching conclusions which stand in striking contrast:

> I have for many years thought that we seek in our mission a great deal too much to make English Christians of our converts … The heathen man is not treated fairly if we encumber our message with unnecessary requirements … We seem to denationalise these races as far as I can see; whereas we ought to change as little as possible – only what is incompatible with the simplest form of teaching and practice …Christianity is the religion for humanity at large. It takes in all shades and characters of race etc.[9]

While Patteson may question the way in which the Christian faith is expressed, never does he doubt the relevance of the Christian message itself. In all of his letters there is a constant longing that Melanesians may know Christ and experience God's promises. Charles Fox notes 'the spirit of prayer' and 'thanksgiving' which pervades all his writings. He is rigorous in his faith too, fearing sentimental attachment which would patronise the converts and overlook the need

7. Ibid., p. 56.
8. Julian Pettifer, *Missionaries*, pp. 20-23
9. Charlotte Yonge, *Life of John Coleridge Patteson*, Macmillan, London, 1874, Vol 2, pp. 164-167
10. Charles Fox, *Lord of the Southern Isles*, p. 19. The motto for St. John's College, New Zealand.

for discipline, 'true religion, sound learning and useful industry.'[10] Neither did he glamorize Melanesian culture or overlook the reality of blood feuds, tribal wars, head-hunting, and pagan practices: he remains totally committed to the mission to 'convert the heathen'.

What becomes increasingly obvious is how personally and intimately he becomes involved in the lives of those he seeks to convert and teach: his missionary methodology is the result of that intimacy. We sense in his letters how much he depends on their reciprocal love and affection. He painfully struggles to make sense of tragic events and his own responsibility for them, and to reconcile this with his faith. For example, in 1863, while he was training Melanesians at St Andrew's, Kohimarama, New Zealand, there was an outbreak of dysentery which took the life of six Melanesian students and made twenty others seriously ill. Patteson attended the sick day and night, and his struggle between grief and faith is captured in a letter to his sister:

> Sosaman died at 4 a.m. this day – a dear lad, one of the Banks Islanders, about ten or twelve years old. As usual I was kneeling close by him, closing his eyes in death. I can see his poor mother's face now! What will she say to me? She knows not the Christian life in death. Yet to him, the poor unbaptised child, what is it to him? There is another world! There is a God, a Father, a Lord Jesus Christ, a Spirit of holiness, a love and glory.[11]

Even harder for Patteson to reconcile was the death of two of his most devoted Norfolk Island assistants, in 1864, when they were fatally wounded in an arrow attack while returning with Patteson from the shore to the ship in Graciousa Bay, Santa Cruz. Patteson writes:

> I never felt so utterly broken down, when I think of the earthly side of it … I long for the sight of his dear face, the sound of his voice. It was my delight to teach him, and he was clever and so thoughtful and industrious. I know that it is good that my affections should be weaned from all things earthly. I try to be thankful. I think I am

11. Yonge, op. cit., vol. II, p. 34.

thankful really; time too will do much. God's grace much more.[12]

It is in moments such as these that we see Patteson's deep humanity breaking through the boundaries of his prescribed faith with which he tries to contain and make sense of his feelings. His deep affection for his Melanesian converts, coupled with a growing sense of isolation from his own culture, leads him increasingly to challenge the missionary attitudes of his day.

It was this humility and genuine concern, witnessed in acts of loving service, that had the power to convert. George Sarawia, who was to be the first Melanesian priest to be ordained, describing Patteson and the missionary model he set, wrote in his autobiography:

> This is what they did for the sick. They were not ashamed to carry the bucket of waste matter and take it to the sea, they washed out the bucket and brought it back into the sick room. Then I thought they were doing what the Bishop had taught us in the school, that we should love one another and look after each other with love, without despising anyone, we should help the weak. All this they did to those who were sick. Then I thought it was true, if anyone taught ... the things that Jesus did he must follow it himself and humble himself.[13]

Where Patteson was nearest the cutting edge of Victorian thought was in the way he believed mission should come about. He passionately believed the initiative for mission should come from the Melanesians themselves and committed himself to their preparation and training which he believed must involve equality and mutual respect. Patteson was convinced that Melanesians could not only become priests but better priests than many of their European counterparts.[14]

On 20 September 1871, Bishop Patteson was murdered with a club used for beating tappa cloth, on the small island of Nukapu. The

12. ibid., p. 78.
13. George Sarawia. *They Came to My Island* (translated and first published in 1968). Melanesian Press.
14. Yonge, op. cit., vol. 2, p. 343.

manner of Bishop Patteson's death and the stories which have grown up around it, have added to his reputation: this story linked his murder on Nukapu with an act of retaliation against labour traders.[15] The memory of Patteson and his way of service has had a tremendous impact on the Church of Melanesia. Today not only do hundreds of Melanesians name their children after him but also their Churches. Thousands attend his feast day, and the people remember him as both saint and martyr. The cross in Nukapu which marks the place where he was killed reads: 'His life was taken by those for whom he would gladly have given it.'

BROTHER INI KOPURIA AND THE MELANESIAN BROTHERHOOD

Ini Kopuria, the founder of the Melanesian Brotherhood, a Solomon Islander, born on Guadalcanal in 1900, was to take this model of incarnational missionary service a stage further.

He was baptised as a child and grew up in the Anglican tradition, attending the Church missionary schools in Pamua and then St. Barnabas College, Norfolk Island. When he left school his teachers wanted him to become a catechist to his own people; instead, he joined the native police force in the service of the British Colonial Government of that time. His work took him all over Guadalcanal, his home island, both around the coastal areas and up into the inland bush villages. Kopuria, however, badly injured his knee while making an arrest, and it was during several months of inactivity in Tulagi Hospital that he received a vision of Christ which made him question the work to which he was called and led him to a life of missionary service.

In 1925 Ini Kopuria founded a Brotherhood for Melanesians and, in consultation with the bishop, prepared a rule of life in which he dedicated his life and land to God, and made three promises of Christian poverty, chastity and obedience. The following year six

---

15. Certainly his death caused sufficient shock in England to mobilise public opinion against the Melanesian labour trade which had become a scandal. In 1872 a bill to control unregulated recruiting of labour was passed by the British Parliament as the Pacific Islands Protection Act.

Brothers also took promises and joined him, and the Melanesian Brotherhood continued to grow.

The purpose of the Brotherhood was evangelistic. Ini believed that the Gospel should be taken out and lived in the remotest islands and villages. He saw the white European missionary model as often drawing converts away from their traditional way of life. He wanted Melanesians to be evangelised, but in a Melanesian way.

> He thought it all wrong that every Melanesian because of his colour should feel inferior to every white man because of his colour. He thought that there was this feeling even within the Mission and the Church itself.[16]

Ini chose a radical approach. He sent his Brothers out, two by two, on mission to all parts of the Solomon Islands. Arriving unarmed, with no food or possessions, in often hostile villages, they aimed to stay and, if they were accepted by the chief and people, live the life of the people in that place – talking, sharing and working together before moving on. He believed that the standard of living of his Brothers should never rise above the standard of living of the people they served.

It was not long before the reputation of the Brothers began to grow. They were prepared to come and stay. They were not frightened of devils and ancestral spirits. Their prayers could drive away fear. People began to speak of the healings and signs they had witnessed and to say that the Brothers or 'Tasiu', as they became known in the Mota language, had *mana* [17] and spiritual power. Many villages were converted by the Brothers; unfortunately, there were not always priests available to follow up this work of primary evangelism.[18]

16. Charles Fox. Extract from *The Southern Cross Log*, January 1946, vol. 52, no 1.
17. Robert Codrington in his book 1891 *The Melanesians,* defined 'mana' thus: 'This is what works to effect everything beyond the ordinary power of men, outside the common practice of nature; it is present in the atmosphere of life, attaches itself to persons and to things. But this power, though itself impersonal, is always connected with some person who directs it. All Melanesian religion consists in getting this Mana for one's self or getting it used for one's benefit.'
18. Charles Fox, *Kakamora*, Hodder and Stoughton, London, 1962, pp. 67-80; also *Lord of the Southern Isles*, pp. 268-272.

Another characteristic of the Melanesian Brotherhood which made it different from European models of religious community was that Brothers only took temporary vows which could be renewed. Brothers who wished to leave the community after a period of service were free to do so; in this way the intention both honoured and respected the call to married life and believed that the period of religious formation and service would not be wasted when the brother was released from the community and returned to his people.

Brother Charles Fox, upon Ini Kopuria's death in 1945, described him thus:

> I think he was one of the ablest Melanesians I have ever known. What things stood out in his character? First, I think his spirituality. Prayer was a real thing for Ini: he was the most reverent Melanesian I have ever met and that is saying a lot. God was in all his thoughts. Second, his joyousness. He was almost always in high spirits, full of fun, full of joy of being alive: it was good to live with him. Third, his deep understanding of the thoughts of Melanesians. At Brothers' meetings when disputes were often hot, Ini always knew who was really in the wrong and generally got that brother to say so. Fourth, his common sense. He always knew what was practicable and kept discussions to that.[19]

The stories of Kopuria reflect this same vitality and joy for life, rooted both in prayer and a down-to-earth commitment to the people. He led by example.

There are many stories which have surrounded the foundation of this community and its growth, some of which became embellished and part of the story-telling tradition with which history is passed on in Melanesia. But the spirit of these stories reflect a similar message: that these local missionaries were loved and respected by the people and in a very real way belonged to them. These were missionaries who were Melanesians and of whom Melanesians were proud. There are stories of the Brothers praying with the sick, carrying the sick down

19. Charles Fox, Extract from *The Southern Cross Log*, January 1946, vol. 52, no. 1.

from mountain villages to clinics, driving out fear and evil spirits, preparing people for Baptism, fishing, planting, building leaf houses, and visiting everywhere. To pick one of many examples, here is one recorded by Charles Fox:

> I remember coasting along the shores of New Britain in the mission ship looking for somewhere to land two Brothers and receiving a refusal at each 'heathen' village until we found one where the people allowed them to stay. I took them ashore and I rowed back to the ship. I watched these two young men standing there with nothing but their haversacks, among a heathen people of whose language they knew not a word, who might easily kill or starve them after we had gone. They were a thousand miles from their own homes and knew that the mission ship would not come back for a year. A year later we called again and found them standing there once more, this time with twenty of the people prepared for Baptism. After some years there were several hundred Christians there.[20]

The Melanesian Brotherhood was not restricted to the Solomon Islands or to one race. By the 1930s they were working in Vanuatu and Fiji, and in 1955 the Melanesian Brotherhood were asked by the Church to go work among the tribes in the New Guinea Highlands; and it was not long before young men from these countries joined the Brotherhood, and the Brotherhood established three 'Regions': Solomon Island Region, Southern Region (Vanuatu and Fiji), and Papua New Guinea Region. From 1975 to 1994 the Melanesian Brotherhood also worked in Northern Queensland in the Diocese of Carpentaria with Australian Aborigines and Torres Strait Islanders. Most recently, they set up two households in Palawan Philippines, working with the Philippine Independent Church, and already have Filipino vocations. Today the Melanesian Brotherhood numbers about 450 brothers and 180 novices.[21]

20. Charles Fox, *The Melanesian Brotherhood*, The Melanesian Mission, London.
21. For discussion of religious life in South Pacific see: Richard Carter: 'Religious Orders and the Development of the Anglican Church in the South Pacific', *Anglicanism a Global Communion*, Mowbray, London, 1998, pp. 45-51.

A MISSIONARY METHOD FROM BELOW

1. Poverty of Spirit

In countries where there is often little chance of formal education above primary school, many of those attracted to religious life may initially be so because it provides opportunity and a way out of the village. The Brotherhood is seen to live a radical and exciting lifestyle, and becoming a Brother provides a young man with the chance for three years of training, the chance to travel to different islands and perhaps even to carry out mission overseas, and win a great deal of respect from the local community. Less than one third of those joining the community at this time have had any secondary education. The waiting lists to join the community are full: each year the community has only space enough to select thirty to forty novices; but many more than that apply.[22] Yet those joining the community know that it will not be an easy life; and those who join simply for self-advancement and who do not grow beyond that stage, do not stay long.

Within the Melanesian Brotherhood there is a simplicity of lifestyle. They have few possessions or luxuries. They are not seen by the outside community to be working for profit. Within their own community resources are limited. More than forty novices, for example, share each humid dormitory, sleeping on mats: they have no shoes, no watches, no property. Most can fit their possessions into one bag. The community eats twice a day: root crops and some vegetables Sometimes, there is a little fish. In the bush areas they can usually find fruit and always there are coconuts. At times, there will be feast days: pigs will be killed and major fishing expeditions will go out – then there will be plenty. At other times, when the floods and rain come, there may be only potatoes or even nothing. The Brotherhood aim to take special care of any guest who arrives at the community, the Brothers

22. The community has resisted setting academic entrance requirements (some of those selected may have had no formal education at all), novices will be selected from each diocese in the Solomon Islands and this selection will be on signs of their calling and faith, experience and skills in all areas of life, church involvement, references and also to try and make sure each tribe, district, language group and island have brothers in the community.

will therefore hold back to make sure all are properly fed before them. Portions are divided and divided again as guests arrive. Often you will notice those who quietly go without, and this is done with no obvious complaint. The community are not advocating deprivation, neither is it glorifying in a spirit of fasting. (When there is plenty the community will eat as if there is no tomorrow.)

The Brothers will tell you there is freedom in this way of life, this lack of grasping – a freedom to accept what the day provides and to embrace both the feast and the famine. The Head Brother said to me, 'It is good that sometimes I learn to go without; we cannot always have what we want, and this way I learn to appreciate what I do have.' It can also lead to a greater awareness of the needs of others.[23]

There is a very real dependence upon God at the heart of this Brotherhood life-style. It is connected in a very holistic way to God and to the community. There is an awareness of dependence on God in the storms, floods and cyclones which can so easily destroy the people's livelihood and homes. There is a deep awareness of God as Brothers set off by canoe for other islands or to fish in rough seas. There are prayers at times of planting and harvesting, for, in a very direct way, God is connected with the food that they will eat: when the harvest fails they know what it means to go without. In this context, the Lord's prayer translated as 'Give us this day our food for today' becomes a radical expression of the need for God's providential care.

There is faith too as a Brother with often little formal education gets up to preach in a church or teach in a school or kneel down at the bed of the sick to pray for healing. The very work of the Brothers as missionaries enables and gives confidence so that shared gifts and talents can grow. This cannot be described simply in terms of individual development: the Brothers and Sisters believe that they are doing the work of God and put their trust in their belief that what God has commanded he will also empower.

The vow of poverty, which all Brothers take, can lead to a to a new

23. Richard Carter. 'The Vow of Poverty in the Third World' *Anglican Religious Communities Year Book, 1999-2000*, Canterbury Press, Norwich.

way of seeing and living, a new scale of values. Youth culture today is increasingly drawing young people away from traditional life-styles in search of work, cash, and the new values of fashion, alcohol, freer sexual relationships, money, and life centred around the town-ships and capital. Vows of poverty, chastity and obedience are a commitment to a very different set of values. Becoming a part of a community, which is a mix of tribal groups, also challenges the prejudice and 'wontok system'[24] which has led to division and mistrust between the different island groups. The decision to become a Brother affects the whole orientation of a person's life. It is a vocation which although one may embark upon it lightly, will ultimately involve personal struggle and the need for personal conver-sion if one is to remain true to the spirit of this calling.

Poverty of spirit does not justify the poverty of real deprivation and must be distinguished from what Gutierrez calls 'the poverty of death.'[25] Such poverty in Melanesia may mean landlessness, precari-ous housing, lack of water or contamination of the supply, disease, malaria and sickness, little access to education, hunger at times of crop failure, and vulnerability to natural disasters like flood and cyclone. Such poverty is poverty without choice; it is a trapped existence in which there seems no escape or hope of transformation. It is a situation wholly contrary to the will of God.

Within the Brotherhood itself the Brothers will experience at times the darkness of that deprivation: they will share the struggles of the local community. They will know the fear of sickness and poor nutrition in the remote areas they are called to serve. They will also live the frustrations of poverty: no access to transportation, lack of resources to get things changed, requests for repairs, building and community projects ignored and turned down, land and new gardens destroyed by flooding after weeks of work. They will at times feel

24. 'Wontok' means literally 'one talk' and is a term used to describe those of the same tribe who speak the same language. In any of the islands there may be as many as three or four different languages spoken. The 'wontok system' is a term used to describe the way those of the same language group are seen to favour one another. It is a system which is seen to lead to prejudice and nepotism.

25. G. Gutierrez, *The Truth Shall Make You Free*, Orbis Books, Mayrknoll NY

powerless, having no cash to implement solutions or alleviate need.

Poverty of spirit stands both in opposition to such poverty but also in solidarity with those who suffer. 'It assumes, voluntarily and out of love, the condition of the needy of the world in order to bear witness to the evil it represents and to spiritual freedom before possessions.'[26] The Brother has no material advantage over those he has been sent to serve, no layer of financial protection: the work he will do or not do in the towns and villages will depend in a very direct way on his faith and his ability to help and inspire the cooperation of the people. It is a mission not of hand-outs but of being present. His life in the community will involve commitment to neighbour, a commitment that acknowledges that the Christian stands where Christ stands and is found where Christ was found: among those in greatest need.

2. The message of the Gospel is inculturated

The inculturation of the Christian message within the life of Melanesian Brotherhood and other religious communities has meant that the agenda, and the methods for achieving the agenda, could come from Melanesians themselves. Such a shift has freed talents and skills which are possessed by the community and which have often remained dormant if an agenda or programme are imposed from above. When organisation is couched in western terms and involves unfamiliar administrative processes, the local community often fails to engage. There is a failure to realise that the community skills many people possess as a natural part of their cultural heritage, may be the very skills required for Christian mission. When the indigenous missionary is able to inculturate the mission, people begin to realise that 'the Word of God belongs to them.'[27]

Another problem which prevents inculturation is that the culture often sees its own forms and expression as inauthentic or unworthy.[28]

24. Archbishop Oscar Romero, op. cit., p. 72

25. Bosch. *Transforming Mission*, p. 453

26. Paulo Freire argues that 'cultural invasion leads to such inauthenticity: In this phenomenon, the invaders penetrate the cultural context of another group, and ignoring the potential of the latter, they impose their own view of the world upon those they invade and inhibit the creativity of the invaded by curbing their expression'. *Pedagogy of the Oppressed*, Penguin Books, Harmondsworth

They believe that the western forms of worship they have adopted have more power. There has been great difficulty, for example, encouraging the local community to adopt the Pidgin Bible as opposed to the English translation, the argument being that the Word in a language they could understand had lost its dignity and mystery.

The Melanesian Brotherhood and other religious orders have been very instrumental in encouraging the process of inculturation to take place. Inculturation is often the by-product of an involvement with the people rather than a conscious target of a programme of action. The Melanesian missionary orders have been able to break through this cultural prejudice by revealing for all to see, hear and witness that the local culture has a great power and beauty to express the nature of God in its own forms. Within the church itself drums and conch shells can replace bells as a call to prayer, processions can be led by pan-pipes, local custom tunes, rhythms and chants can bring new life to liturgy. Custom dancing has entered the Church as an expression of thanksgiving. God begins to speak the language of the people. Once the power and vitality of indigenous culture has been released few would question its authenticity.

Yet this inculturation also extends far beyond the church building so that the boundaries of the Christian faith can become inclusive of the lives people actually live. If the missionary does not make the move to inculturate, then the Gospel can easily become confined to the mission station. If, on the other hand, the Christian message merges so completely into a culture that it loses its own identity, then the Gospel does not reach the people either, or the Gospel becomes simply a superstitious or cult practice:

> Inculturation does not mean that culture is to be destroyed and something new built up on its ruins; neither, however, does it suggest that a particular culture is merely to be endorsed in its present form ... The philosophy that 'anything goes' as long as it seems to make sense to people, can be catastrophic. In a very real sense the Gospel is foreign to every culture.[29]

29. Bosch, *Transforming Mission.* p. 455.

The Gospel will then at times come into conflict with the culture and must seek to maintain its prophetic voice. This has been very obvious in a number of important social issues: it is the religious communities and the Mothers Union who have consistently spoken out against domestic violence, for example. They have confronted very directly the use of magic and poison which still creates fear within the islands, a process the Brotherhood calls 'clearance'. It was also the religious communities who were brave enough to continue to speak out against inter-island ethnic tension and to oppose that ethnic violence in a very tangible way. They have also helped bring the issues of AIDS and Street Children on to the Church agenda.

3. It is mission for community by community

Western evangelistic missionary approaches have often focused on the conversion of the individual. In their preaching they have constantly stressed the need for a 'personal relationship' with Christ. Gutierrez warns against what he claims can become 'the privatisation of spirituality.' [30] The rapid increase of new denominations and sects entering into Melanesia on the pretext of evangelisation, has divided villages, parishes and communities, throughout the Islands. They have stressed a holiness code in which the individual convert, who is often re-baptised by the new Church, separates himself or herself from the rest of the community, claiming that they have now entered into a true relationship with Christ. Such a missionary approach has naturally given rise to great animosity.

The missionary method of the Melanesian Brotherhood has always been aimed at the whole community. Not only does the Melanesian Brotherhood aim to go to the whole community but to go *as* community. In this, the missionary acknowledges his or her own need for solidarity and dependence upon the combined gifts of the group. An often repeated Solomon Island proverb is that one piece of fire-wood cannot make a fire; many pieces are needed to make the fire burn. A community acknowledges that talents are not in competition with one another but are there to be shared. A community is full of diverse

30. Gustavo Gutierrez, *We Drink from Our Own Wells*, SCM Press, Lonmdon, 1984, p. 15

talents. Once these are offered to the whole group without the need to compete, there is so much more to offer and appreciate in others: some may have gifts of preaching, others of music, of teaching, of planting, of fishing, of building, of organising etc. A community evangelised by a community frees very exciting reciprocal possibilities. The mission witnesses to unity, not just in word but by its very being: it witnesses to the sharing of gifts, it can become a work force, a performing group, a worshipping community.

4. *The missionary expresses his love in giving*

The vow of poverty is not a negative vow of deprivation; it is an openness to all one's neighbours and a readiness to share. In traditional Melanesian culture, people and relationships are nearly always more important than one's own plans and programmes. Part of the life of poverty will involve being open and ready for others when they come and welcoming them with the generosity of Christ, however inconvenient the requests may be.

Giving is also reciprocal. The missionary is supported by the local community. All these religious communities have local supporters, associates called 'Companions', who promise to support the communities financially, in prayer and in kind. If this support is not forthcoming they know that the community will go without and suffer. This arrangement has encouraged local people to take a very real interest in their support. To deprive someone of the ability to share and be generous is one of the greatest forms of deprivation in our modern society. When Jesus said that it was better to give than to receive he was not expressing a moral code but a simple truth. By realising that the missionary needs the support of the people the poorest of villagers themselves can become the hosts and the greatest generosity and joy is often found at the homes of those who have least.

5. *The Brotherhood is inclusive*

The fact that the Brotherhood is open to all tribes, islands and nations has meant that they have been able to be inclusive in a way that many local communities are not. It sets out rules within its community to prevent island or tribal divisions emerging within the community.

All twenty-seven of the Brotherhood households within the Solomon Islands, for example, are mixed according to language-group and island-origin. When they are together it is the rule that all Brothers speak the common language of 'pidgin'. Sharing everything, it is hoped the bond of their Christian community will bind them together, even when there is prejudice and division in the wider society.

The strength of this approach was witnessed during ethnic tensions and fighting in the Solomon Islands from 1998 to 2000 between the people of Guadalcanal and Malaita. The religious communities remained the only ones trusted by both sides. Their communities became refuges for Malaitan refugees; and later, when Malaitans controlled Honiara the capital, the religious communities were the only groups who had freedom of movement to provide essential supplies for Guadalcanal. It was the Brothers, too, who were able to negotiate with militants to secure the release of hostages. In May 2000 the Brotherhood sent out four groups of Brothers who camped in the no-man's land between enemy lines for the next five months, preaching and living a message of forgiveness and non-retaliation.

The Head Brother, Harry Gereniu, spoke of the need for the religious communities to show their own community solidarity as a sign of the Christian hope and reconciliation which their mission must work to extend from their households to the whole nation. Within the religious communities themselves, Malaitans and Guadalcanal continued to live and work side by side. When a peace settlement was signed in Townsville, Australia, those involved in the conflict acknowledged the role of the indigenous religious communities whose brothers and sisters

> ... have shown amazing courage, literally putting themselves in the cross fire and going backwards and forwards across the lines to try to reduce tension and bring comfort and support to villagers in the battle zone. Wherever there is an incident they are quickly on the scene.[31]

31. John Pinder, 'Where Religious Orders are Maintaining Order' *Church Times*, 2~ October 2000

On 7 July 2001 the Solomon Islands Government acknowledged the contribution the Brothers had made by awarding twenty-one Brothers medals 'for dedicated service and bravery during the tension.'

6. There is creativity

The missionary approach, while living out its tradition, must always be responsive to all forms of creativity: drama, art, music, dance, building, gardening, carpentry, carving, comedy, the beauty of place and environment. It must encourage the full release of the potential of all involved. It should in this way encourage experimentation, with no fear of failure, and yet, at the same time, aim to express, with quality and with truthfulness, the themes with which it is involved. Creativity is one of the most essential paths to conversion.

Within the Melanesian Brotherhood, dance and drama and music have become a vital part of the liturgy, and thus liturgy can be expressed, not in the voice of another culture, but with one's own voice and the instruments of one's own people. In drama, parable, story, dance and music, the story of Christ can become the people's own story, and the hero one of them. In creative mission the players are pulled into the event. A time past can become their own and the response to that story can become a decision for the present.

In the Melanesian Brotherhood's missions, drama has also played a vital part, for it crosses barriers and expresses truths in many-sided ways which teaching finds it hard to encompass. Drama as a method for mission can lead people to a new stance towards their lives, requiring that they question what they see: at its best, it can cut across stereotypes and prejudice and constantly require that the spectator respond. In good drama the audience are not given a message but can discover new meaning for themselves. It has particular relevance in a culture where there is not high adult literacy and where Christian teaching may sometimes seem too abstract and obscure. Drama has great power to lead people to deep questioning and transformation.

A dramatisation of *The Good Samaritan,* for example, was performed around Guadalcanal during the period of ethnic violence there. With the militants standing round with guns, the parable confronted the people with a Malaitan, their enemy, beaten up by militants and left dying on the road; they witnessed the priest walking by and refusing to get involved; and then the Government military in pursuit of the militants but refusing to stop; and then an old man from their own tribe, speaking the home-language of the audience, hearing cries in a different language, the language of his enemy, stopping, bending down, gently cleaning away the blood and binding the wounds and then picking up the Malaitan and carrying him to safety. There was total silence, a deathly silence, when you knew a whole, huge crowd was listening to every sound: a tension so great that one feared the audience may suddenly attack the actors, and one no longer knew whether they saw the Good Samaritan as saviour or traitor. 'Which of these was a true neighbour?' Some of the audience began to sob. The militants who were watching stayed until the end and then quietly disappeared into the night, perhaps carrying this parable with them.

This event touched the wound of ethnic hatred and cried out for a similar healing, and it was only the audience who could make that possible. It was a time when moralistic teaching would never have been heard; but the parable, as story and action, slipped past their defences. Christ's subversive message of love and forgiveness of enemies as the only means of reconciliation had been brought radically alive.

DIFFICULTIES

As Melanesian society develops materially – with the rise of a cash economy and much larger urban culture and cultural freedom – there is increased temptation for Brothers to abandon their vows of poverty, chastity and obedience. When one Brother transgresses the rule it is often the whole Brotherhood which is blamed. This obviously has both advantages and disadvantages. It is perhaps one of the hidden strengths of religious life that it must witness not only in times of achievement and success but also witness to Christ when facing up to the weaknesses and errors of its own members.

Perhaps the greatest question of all facing the Brotherhood is, like religious communities before it, how to cope with its own growth, success and development, without losing touch with its spiritual roots which are its greatest strength. Increasingly, the Brotherhood is being called upon to lead mission further afield and to organise itself in a way that will be able to mission on a much wider level. Missions in the modern world have also needed organisation, administrative and financial skills and the need for more training and thus more expenditure. As mission has increased and gone further afield, the Brothers have needed to consider more income-generating projects to support that outreach and more outside financial support from supporters and overseas Churches. The future of the Brotherhood will depend on how well they will be able to balance that need for resource and manpower development with that 'poverty of spirit' which is so essential to their missionary calling.

A MISSION FOR THE WIDER CHURCH

Bishop George Augustus Selwyn wrote in 1854: 'as running water purifies itself, so Christian work is seen to correct its own mistakes. Is it then a hope too unreasonable to be entertained, that the power which will heal the divisions of the Church at home may come from her distant mission fields?'[32]

There has been much talk in recent mission circles of the need to encourage reverse mission, not simply one-way mission from the North to South, but from the South to the North, from the 'Third World' to the 'First World'. If partnership in mission is going to do more than simply alleviate a guilty conscience for past missionary failures then, argues Andrew Kirk, it is vital that 'the communities in the South share in person with communities in the North, their gifts and understanding of mission in the way of Christ.'[33] For the millennium year 2000, such a mission approach was carried out by the Melanesian Brotherhood in three different new cultural contexts:

32. G. H. Curteis, *Bishop Selwyn of New Zealand and Lichfield*, 1889, London, p. 152
33. Andrew Kirk, *What Is Mission?*, 1999, p.204.

New Zealand, the UK, and the Philippines. The Melanesian Brotherhood set out to respond to these requests using its own missionary
approach. But what could they offer?

The missionaries were young. It was a fact often commented on by
the host community that those leading the mission, 18-30 year-old
men, were the age group most lacking from the Anglican Church in
the 'developed world' The missionaries did not belong to any one
faction within the Church. The fact that they were all missionaries
from the other side of the world allowed them to break through
prejudices and boundaries that often divide the Church. There was a
confidence in faith in marked contrast to many of those they met who
seemed disillusioned and cynical about the Church. They believed
that God was at the centre of their lives and that prayer was an essential
part of their day.

But this faith was expressed naturally without fanaticism or judgement. There was no pretence or affectation and no inhibitions about
sharing with people from all backgrounds: the homeless, in the
prisons, with young people and teenagers. The cultural differences
projected them into a greater honesty and intimacy without fear of
judgment.

The Brothers were able to express their faith in the vitality of
worship. Frequently they were able to break through the rigidity and
formalism of English Church tradition while not appearing to threaten
those who valued those traditions. It allowed the host community to
relax and to participate at a deep level. It was both teaching and
learning, giving and taking. It was a mission which entered into
dialogue with the host community. Both those on mission and those
welcoming mission were interacting, learning about one another and
learning about God. It was a missionary group not seeking to compete:
it acknowledged and yet was unashamed of its own inexperience and
dependence on the gifts of others. It did not try to impose its own view
or way of doing things but simply offered in humility the faith gifts of
its community.

It was a new voice, a voice and an expression which had not been

seen or heard before in the UK. It was the first time many congrega-
tions had heard an eighteen year-old preach, for example, or had heard
Pacific pan-pipes or witnessed Melanesian worship and celebration or
type of drama. The mission was able to break through the confines of
culture to see with new eyes a faith in God not on the peripheries of
life but at its centre.

In the Church of Melanesia the Melanesian Brotherhood has been
able to witness to the possibilities of a mission, which at its heart aims
at exchange and relationship. It is a mission which does not begin from
above but from below and which can empower both the missionary
and the one to whom the missionary is sent. This mission at its best can
create a new sense of belonging and sharing with one another, a new
sense of community.

SIX

Reflections on the Vowed Life:

Commitment through Celibacy

STEPHANIE THÉRÈSE SLG

In a society that champions independence and self-gratification with a reality that is sometimes virtual, where materials and often relationships are disposable and responsibilities transitory, why do men and women enter the religious life and commit themselves for life under vows, and seemingly turn their backs on the wealth of opportunities that life has to offer? The story is different for each person who makes this choice, but the origins of the vowed life are found in an awakening.

The vowed life is based on and anchored in the Great Commandment: 'You shall love the Lord your God with all your heart, and with all your soul and with all your mind. This is the great and first commandment. And the second, you shall love your neighbour as yourself.' (Mt 22:37-39) There are three elements to the commandment: loving God, loving neighbour, and loving self. Because the commandment is concerned with love, it is concerned with relationships – right relationship with God, right relationship with neighbour, and right relationship with self. The vowed life helps us to focus our efforts to maintain a proper balance in these 'right relationships of love.' The Benedictine vows of stability, conversion of manners and obedience predate the today more common medieval vows of poverty, chastity and obedience, but both sets of vows strikingly illustrate this idea of balance and right relationship as the diagram on the following page shows.

In monastic teaching the 'self' has tended to be denied or ignored, sometimes in wholly unhealthy ways, but by including this previously negated and neglected self in one's relationships and love, a space is

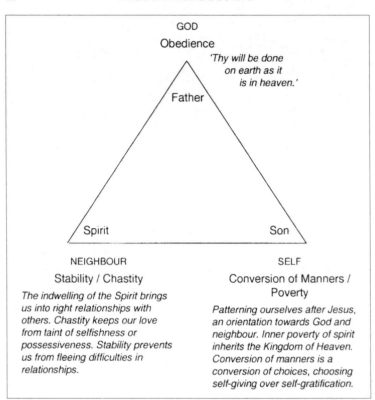

opened up.[1] There must be space in relationships and the means of love if the whole Body of Christ with all its constituent parts is to become that for which God has created it. The vows enable us to engage in the process of becoming, revealing the image of God in which we are all made. This becoming is a state of constant growth and change and renewal, inwardly, outwardly, individually, corporately. 'Behold, I make all things new.' (Rev 21:5) Our choice in making religious vows orientates our self to God and to neighbour in a special way.

---

1. The Great Commandment is often regarded on twofold and linear terms of the vertical (= love of God) and of the horizontal (= love of neighbour). There seems to be no reciprocity as well as no space in this approach, though there is a lot of action which can be assumed to be positive and fruitful outwards from the individual (self).

VOWED TO GOD

The triangle in the figure brings also to mind the Trinity, and this is not irrelevant. For it is the Trinity, God the Father, God the Son, and God the Holy Spirit, to whom we vow ourselves. The vows are not to a human person or an institution but to God. It is true the vows are made in and through an institution, a religious community within the Church, and that they are received by a person, in some cases a bishop or priest, in others the superior of the community, but the vows are actually made to God.

We vow ourselves to God in and through the community/church, which as Paul says is the Body of Christ. Commenting on the Body in 1 Corinthians 12:18, Paul writes, 'As it is, God has put all the separate parts into the body *as he chose.*' (NJB) Paul knew that our faith and our commitment to God comes not from our own initiation, but in *response* to God's love for and his seeking after us shown through the incarnation of his Son, Jesus Christ. God chooses us, calls us, and we respond. Our responding involves a discernment of how God has placed us in the Body. 'I have called you by name and you are mine.' (Is 43:1)

Every Christian vocation on one level is a very personal, singular affair. We are all individually called, but we must each discern our place in relationship to others within the Body of Christ. For we are never called to a life in isolation from others. Some of us discern a call to life under monastic vows. We respond by joining a religious community, therein finding the place God has chosen for us in his Body.

God calls us by speaking to us through his Word, his Son Jesus Christ. Through the Incarnation, God shows us in the substance of our own human flesh, how to respond to Him. God's word is love, and our response is love to the Original Love. God the Father calls us through his Son who shows us by word and example how to respond, and he gives us through the Holy Spirit the energy and power to respond. This love emphasizes the reciprocity in the relationship we make in vowing ourselves to God. This is not a disinterested partner with whom we are engaging: He gives us not only word and example in a form with which we are familiar, the human life and death of Jesus, but also power in his Holy Spirit which enables our response.

To vow ourselves to God is not a passive act on our part either. A vocation is given to us, but it is not done for us. It is our choice to respond to God's call. We freely reach out our hands to receive God's gift, and in order to grasp the wholeness of what we are offered, our 'hands' need to be empty. So the vowed life is simply one expression of that reaching out of ourselves to receive what God longs to give to us, his children. In making vows we are making an outward sign of an inward movement of response, a response initiated by an encounter with love.

Monastic vows are not made in isolation or privately. Christianity, though a religion of Mystery, is not a secretive religion. We do not hide the Truth from others, we witness to it. Our vowed life is a form of witness, a silent witness perhaps because we live the vows, we do not (or should not) preach the vows. Silent but not secret. 'The works of God should be acknowledged publicly.' (Tob 12:7) The vows aid us in keeping our hands empty to receive, our hearts open to give God opportunity to do his work in and through us. 'There are many different ways of serving, but it is always the same Lord. There are many different forms of activity, but in everybody it is the same God who is at work in them all.' (1 Cor 12:5.6)

AN EXPRESSION OF COMMITMENT

The vowed life is an expression of commitment to God in all aspects of, and in every moment in our life. One does not need to become a monk or nun to live a life fully committed to Christ. It is simply one way to live the Christian commitment, but it is a way that provides fellowship and encouragement, guidance as well as an accountability, not in a punitive sense but an enabling accountability.

The vows are what we make them. They are tools in the hands of a craftsman. They can build barriers and scaffolding or ladders and bridges. The choice is ours. To fully live out our vows, engaging in our relationships to God and to others, will enable us to become that specific individual person God has called into being when we were born. There is a choice to make vows and a daily choice to live the vows. What influences the choices we make is the underlying trust in and commitment to the monastic life and vows as a means to seek and serve God. Only in giving ourselves completely to the life we have undertaken in vows will we experience true self-fulfilment. Only the empty vessel can be filled. It is one of the paradoxes of the vowed life – the simultaneous, if not symbiotic, emptying of self and indwelling of God.

AN EXPRESSION OF LOVE

Love is not inert. It is dynamic and seeks expression. To pattern our love after God's love is to nurture right relationships with God, with our neighbour and with our self. These relationships are self-aware and self-giving but not selfish or possessive. Our love for God is our faith and trust in the Father. Paul uses the word 'love' (*agape*) to refer to God's relationship to us and our relationship to others. He rarely uses the word *agape* in terms of our relationship to God. Instead Paul speaks of our relationship to God in terms not of love but of faith. Our right relationship with God is faith: we love God not by believing *in* him but by *believing him.*

Our right relationship with others, though, must reflect God's relationship to us manifested in his Son Jesus Christ. But how? Here the apostles teach us. John writes, 'God is love. In this the love of God was made manifest, that God sent his only Son into the world, so that we might live through him.' (1 Jn 4:8b.9) Paul writes, 'Have this mind among yourselves, which is yours in Christ Jesus' (Phil 2:5); and to the Corinthians he writes the famous passage: 'Love is patient and kind, love is not jealous or boastful; it is not arrogant or rude. Love does not insist on its own way; it is not irritable or resentful; it does not rejoice at wrong, but rejoices in the right. Love bears all things, believes all things, hopes all things, endures all things.' (1 Cor 13:4-7) Substitute your own name for 'love' in the First Corinthians passage. This is what the vowed life should enable us to do: to become 1 Corinthians 13:4-7.

An Oblate Sister wrote to me at my profession, 'The same for the Sister as for the virtuoso musician: more devotion, dedication, and practice, practice, practice.' Love requires practice as well as encouragement and lots of effort, a lifetime of it, in fact. For the monk and nun community provides the environment for that practice. Our primary relationships should be found within the community in our worship of God in the Eucharist and the Divine Office, and in our relationships with our sisters and brothers. However wide our nets are cast, we are related most closely with the others in our community, together vowed to God through the Rule of the community. For how can we witness in our outreach to God's love and forgiveness with any honesty if we are unable to show the same enthusiasm and love within our community relationships?

Making vows does not change a person; it is the living out of the vows in community that changes us and brings us closer to the One whom we seek. The vowed life is a journey, and it is the journey that changes you. Our outreach and ministry along the way is the overspill of the indwelling Spirit. The vows help us through discipline and self-awareness (self-knowledge) to empty ourselves of selfishness in order to be filled to overflowing with the Spirit of God's love. The more we empty, the more we overflow, the more we serve! It is not a matter of being home free once you make your vows, it is a matter of every day beginning again on the journey from where you are, to seek God with all your heart, with all your mind, with all your soul and with all your strength.

LIVING THE VOWS

The community provides the space for learning and living the experience of the vowed life. As with any endeavour, there will be planned and unplanned diversions, mishaps and accidents, occasional disasters, hard work, sometimes boredom, sometimes loneliness. But there will be as well the wonder of the sought-after and the unexpected. Each community will have its own Rule and complementary documents expounding their own ethos and expression of the religious life. The Rule often addresses the larger truths of the life, such as the vows, the sacraments, disciplines of silence and prayer. The details of daily living can be found – if written out at all – in a document often called a Customary. The Customary earths our vows into the daily life and activities. Different generations prefer varying degrees of detail in the exposition of the Rule or vows. For most of the twentieth century, certainly before Vatican II, the expression of our vows tended towards highly ordered systems of behaviour. The vows remained the same – poverty, chastity and obedience in most cases – but the local customs and traditions passed down with 'The Great Tradition' were often very exact (and exacting), the details taking so much time and attention that sometimes the inspiration could die. Here we see the constant battle between 'the law and the spirit.' Getting the right balance between letter and spirit is crucial to the vowed life, because both aspects are important. It is easy to fall prey to the letter and law in a highly regulated system. So, the religious must always be vigilant.

It is good to remember the Pharisees at this point. The Pharisees extended the priestly code of conduct to the entire people. They practised the purity laws of Torah as if they were temple priests themselves, taking in a very literal sense the text 'you shall be a kingdom of priests and a holy people.' (Ex 19:6) The Pharisees formed closed communities, and membership was a matter of initiation into the *haburah* or fellowship in which the individual undertook to follow certain obligations. They had popular support among the masses even though their membership was limited, and were known for their simple living, their fasting and tithing, their strict Sabbath observances, and their warmth of devotion. They made the Law relevant to current circumstances; their religion was not just in the Temple but in every aspect of daily living. (Sound familiar?) The trap of this extensive ritualisation of daily life is legalism, the chief accusation against the Pharisees in the Gospels (e.g. Luke 11:42-44).

We may not meticulously tithe mint and rue, but for those of us who take on board disciplines above and beyond the ordinary, it would be wise to pay attention to Jesus' warning to the Pharisees. He is speaking to us. If we get ensnared in scrupulosity, our disciplines can lead us away from what we seek instead of towards it. When our customs and disciplines, the details of our lifestyle, are kept in proportion to their purpose, the spirit of the vows will be safeguarded.

It all comes back again to balance, to perspective, to balancing the letter and the spirit: unless the spirit of the vows is internalized and lived, the letter of the rule will become nothing more than a new Law. So we must heed Jesus' warning to the Pharisees, for the snare of legalism can easily entrap us, too. The letter without spirit is legalism, but the spirit without the letter is a trap as well. There must be definition and boundaries to our actions. Extremes are best avoided. Extremes may be noticeable, but to whom or to what are they witnessing?

We need to keep a healthy perspective between the customs of the past and the needs of the present. There should be a healthy tension between letter and spirit, especially where inherited customs and present circumstances meet. They are reconcilable if they interact, but not if they stand in isolation one from the other or are imposed one on another. It seems obvious, but sometimes needs to be said out loud, that the present should not be held hostage to our past, and neither should the past be ignored or dismissed for it is a treasure of teaching and wisdom for today.

We need to maintain right relationships toward God, our neighbour, and ourself. The triangle in the diagram (p. 92) is equilateral, with God at its top and converging point. The space in the triangle suggests the space there should be in relationships to allow all to become who they are meant to be in relationship to the others. We are reminded by the triangle that we are as close to God as to our neighbour, and that each neighbour is as close to God as we are.

THE VOWS

There are many very good and detailed books about the vows, and it is not the purpose of this essay to explore the individual vows in depth. The following paragraphs are simply short reflections from my experience of living the vowed life for nearly fifteen years in a contemplative religious community.

Poverty

Monastic poverty is not about penury and rarely today does it mean you go without necessary things. Externally, monastic poverty is seen in a radical simplification of lifestyle; but, internally, it is the recognition of our entire dependence on God for all things. In our individualistic and independent culture, dependence is not seen as a positive characteristic. But dependence on God means believing and trusting that all real needs will be met by him. Monastic poverty involves a discipline of discerning needs from wants, and detaching ourselves from always wanting to possess things or people, or privileges. When the discernment between needs and wants is seriously undertaken, one begins to realise how few our essential needs actually are and how frequently and generously they are met.

As with all spiritual disciplines, the external expressions of the vow of poverty are undertaken to nurture and strengthen the internal grace and spirit of poverty. The action of our choices reflects the intention of our hearts, the channelling of our attention and effort towards God, towards our neighbour, or towards ourself. To choose for self is not always greed or selfishness, but we must be vigilant, for it is easy to be deceived by our wants.

In the past many communities had very strict practices imposed on everyone in regard to poverty. A generation's culture might become embedded in a community's practices of poverty as well. Having been born in the 1950s and raised in America, I often wondered in my early days in community here in England how many of our practices were left over patterns from the war years and rationing, and how much they really had to do with 'poverty'. A very small example: Is poverty about set routines such as meticulously scraping margarine papers and rinsing milk bottles, or is it a mindfulness about not being wasteful?

Today the spirit of the vow of poverty is encouraged throughout our life, more so than legislating possessions, procedures, and personal choices. This means the individual takes on a greater responsibility and maturity in living the vow of poverty. The more freedom one has, the greater the need for discernment at a personal level. This shift has also brought a new diversity into the common life. In days gone by, our vow of poverty was expressed in conformity – the same dress, the same food, the same prayer times, and such like. Today, our poverty is seen still in simplicity, but less in sameness.

Poverty also impinges on the stewardship of our resources. Does poverty *always* mean buying the cheapest, or does it involve buying ethically when and where possible? Do we buy the cheapest fabric for our habits or more expensive material that will still be wearing well after ten or more years? With fewer numbers in community a real aspect of our poverty today is managing time. There now may not be time to scrape all those margarine papers and get dinner on the table with three or four fewer sisters in the kitchen.

We must discern poverty corporately as well as individually. Poverty without choice, poverty by rote no longer seems to inspire those entering today. They ask: Why do we do this? What does it mean? We need to be able to answer them. For those of us who have been around a while, poverty may be asking us to live in a whole new way, to give up the familiar and possibly much loved older customs. However poverty is expressed, it will always remain costly.

Chastity

When I was very new to religious life, an elderly sister in an active community told me about her early days in community. I was fascinated. Then the long habit sleeves down to the fingertips were meant to hide the hands. She had been expressly taught to keep her hands out of sight so as not to attract attention to herself. (This sister even in her 70s had noticeably beautiful hands, now visible in the shorter wrist-length sleeves of the modern habit.) They also were not allowed out alone, but must always be in pairs when outside the convent. A sister had to ride in the back seat of a car if the driver were male, even if he were her father or brother. And never were they to eat or drink in public. To my baby-boomer ears, these customs sounded ridiculous, like left-overs from some Victorian ideal of female modesty. But for her, they were formative experiences in living out her vow of chastity as a young nun.

More recently, a sister said to me that one of her students had asked her, 'Why would anyone want to take a vow of chastity today?' She admitted that she did not have a satisfactory answer, and, on short notice, neither did I. On reflection, I began to wonder if the student might have been asking, 'Why would anyone want to live without sex?' I may have gotten it wrong, but the vow of chastity is frequently confused with celibacy, which is one of the external disciplines of monastic chastity. So what is chastity about?

Chastity concerned the passions, but it is about purity of heart. 'Blessed are the pure in heart for they shall see God.' (Mt 5:8) Through chastity, a person sets their attentions fully on God, where body, mind and spirit are purified in Christ. Chastity is like a prism through which the passions are passed and broken down into their constituent parts, seen in their true colours. Chastity is about the purification of those passions, not their suppression. Lust is but one of the passions. We need also to purify our greed, our anger, our impatience, our selfishness, our possessiveness, and all the other emotions that interfere with our relationships. Purified passions are still there within us, but they do not dissipate or exhaust our energy.

By focusing and channelling the passions Godwards, the mind, body and spirit are transformed and begin to see God in all things. The primary place where God is seen by the pure in heart is in our neighbour. Nothing will more quickly blind our eyes to the image of God in another than our own disordered passions. Our right relationship with our neighbour is essentially only possible through chastity. With mind, body and spirit wholly set on God we will be able to see the image of God in our neighbour, to love them as God's own, and to forgive that which might blur his image, because we know that that is how God looks on us.

The passions need continual purification because there will always be parts of us unfocused and unredeemed, parts which are thrown up in every new circumstance and relationship. Chastity, when considered as purity of heart, is taken out of the sole domain of monastic life and into the lives of all Christians. We are all called by God to live a chaste life, and some of us choose to express it through the discipline of celibacy within the context of a religious community. Chastity seeks to express the right ordered relationships of a pure heart.

Obedience

A few years ago I was chatting with a novice sister about how much change there had been in community since I had joined not so many years earlier. Talking about small things, I mentioned that when I was a novice (grating words to every novice's ears, I'm sure), we had only been allowed two cups of coffee a day, one after Mass and another in the afternoon, a big adjustment for someone coming from coffee-saturated America as I did. The novice responded with, 'Nobody's going to tell me how many cups of coffee I can drink!' I pointed out that I did not think that was what it was all about, then chuckled and added, 'If you think self discipline is so easy, you should try drinking only two cups of coffee a day!'

To me it is an interesting episode because all the vows seem to come into play. The quantity of coffee and its expense touches on the vow of poverty, the discipline of the appetite (or, in my case, blatant greed) for coffee on the vow of chastity. But the novice's response is interesting because obedience is *not* about being told what to do. If poverty guards our stewardship, and chastity our passions, obedience then is the guardian of our will.

Our obedience reinforces the utter dependence on God in the vow of poverty, and it orders our passions in the vow of chastity. Rightly, it sits at the pinnacle of the triangle with God the Father (p. 92). Obedience will always require our best effort because it directly counters that first temptation in the Garden of Eden inherent in each human soul, the serpent's 'you will be like God.' Jesus does not tempt us with divinity. He redeems us and gives us eternal life in the Trinity. Through the gospel of Jesus Christ we *can* come to know good from evil. Over and over again, Jesus' obedience points to the Father's will. 'For I have come down from heaven, not to do my own will, but the will of him who sent me.' (Jn 6:38)

Through Jesus' self-emptying (Phil 2:5-11) he exercised obedience to the Father. Imagine how costly the obedience of the Incarnation was for God the Son – he let go of the privileges and rights of equality with God! It must have been like losing an entire dimension to one's being. Would it be like us trying to live in a two-dimensional world when our nature demands three? I personally cannot imagine any obedience requiring that much from me. But embracing the imitation of Christ's self-emptying is necessary for us all if we want to be filled with the fullness of God. Through our obedience we re-establish our will to be one with the will of God, Jesus being our teacher and our example.

In the United Kingdom and other mainstream democratic cultures, our obedience rarely demands Christ's 'even unto death'. Still, we always have to pray with Jesus in Gethsemane: 'Not my will but thine be done.' Obedience *is* about self-denial and self-loss, but it is not about self-annihilation. It is not a means to punish ourselves out of existence because of our sins. God's promise is fullness of life, that total abundance which only he can give. We cannot manufacture it, but we can prepare to receive it by making room for God's indwelling. We must empty ourselves of that false self, the one who wants to be in control, at the centre of attention, calling the shots. When the false self goes, the true self can be expressed – that unique individual who we are, made in the image of God.

Our obedience in community is earthed in the ordinary tasks of everyday living. When we join a community, we opt into a system of customs and expected behaviour. Our obedience to the customs and traditions of our community is a real discipline of self-emptying. Nobody finds everything to their liking, and it is often the smallest things that require so much struggling and yielding. What may seem like petty legislated details, when explored can reveal the truths of the monastic way tested over the centuries yet found in the small details of the life. Those two cups of coffee did have a lot to do with the learning of self-discipline and self-control. If you practise with the small things, you can manage when the large, more crucial challenges are encountered. Our obedience should enable us to overcome our tendency to self-please and encourage within us habits that turn us towards God. If they do not, or if the teaching has become completely detached from the situation, then we need to reassess our customs. Sometimes we will simply have to do what we are told, and it may require our greatest trust that God is in it all somewhere, even if we can not perceive him. I doubt there is a community that does not have a clause about conscientious objection within the rule. If obedience is forced, it is not obedience but coercion. But when freely entered into and offered, obedience in the small details as well as the great gestures, is the single most efficient discipline in transforming our likeness into Christ's.

CHANNELLING OUR ENERGY

'I believe that without the impetus of love it is not possible to begin or continue any journey of the spirit. But love, too, must know its measure and its limitations.' [2] It is true that we limit ourselves in making vows. We freely do this in order to make ourselves more available to God in order for God to work his will in and through us. So, is the proverbial glass of water half empty or half full? The vows can be seen as restrictive, a taking away of a person's liberty to do whatever he or she wants. Or the limitations can be understood as a means of unencumbering oneself with worldly demands and expectations in order to be more encumbered with the ways of God. A simplistic comparison and limited by the fact that it tends towards the externals; but, unfortunately, this is often how the religious life is

2. Quotation attributed to Sister Thekla and found in *From a Monastery Kitchen* (revised edition), by Brother Victor-Antoine d'Avila-Latourrette, Triumph Books, Liguori, Missouri), ca 1989, p. 56.

perceived and understood at large – by the externals. Unless the externals witness to a profound inner transformation of the person, are they anything more than sham or prop? 'The habit gives the appearance of holiness but not the virtue.' We are vowed, not to keeping rules or to continuing specific mission work or to maintaining a quaint old-fashioned lifestyle, but to witnessing prophetically to the transforming, liberating, and self-fulfilling love of the Father.

If monastic externals are misunderstood or are confusing to either ourselves or outsiders, then we need to ask ourselves: Why? What are our energies consumed with, what are we witnessing to? Like all Christians, religious are called to respond to God's love in faith and action, to be stewards of both his tangible and intangible gifts to us. This requires vigilance and discernment on our parts, both as individuals and as communities. The stewardship demanded by the vowed life involves stewardship of the commitment, the vision and the mission as well as stewardship of the community, both the members and the physical plant(s). In the latter half of the twentieth century, so often the size and commitments demanded by our sites and ministries have overtaken the number and strength of the community's membership. An imbalance has occurred where the externals of 'keeping the show going' demand most of our energy and overstretch us to the point where discernment can become impaired. Discernment is ongoing. It is not a one-off decision to enter the religious life or to undertake a specific work, but a continual discernment of how to respond to God in the present circumstances. Here the vows give us a framework with which to discern and to respond because they constantly return our gaze to God. As for the individual, so for the community.

We have vowed ourselves to God, both individually and corporately, to grow and mature into Christ, not to produce quantifiable 'good works'. A challenge today is not letting the traditional work and routines of our communities overwhelm the vision and the mission. There must be an external expression of that vision, but the 'what' and the 'why' must be kept in balance. The vowed life must never be used to maintain the *status quo*; it must ever be the challenge and the goad and the means to seek God.

For, put as simply as possible, the vowed life is one dedicated to seeking God at all costs, letting go of much good the world and society have to offer, in order to grasp the Good above all else. Our vows should keep us ready to receive the new and the unexpected, not always what we would choose, but in God's wisdom what is needed to be drawn closer to him. This abandonment to the spirit of the vows takes courage and faith, for believing God is much, much more than believing in God. And God knows the difficulty for us. For how many times throughout the Scriptures does he say to us, 'Be not afraid, fear not'?

How do we seek God? By imitating Christ. We feed the poor, tend the sick, visit those in prison; we proclaim the Good News not only from pulpit, but today often through retreats, spiritual direction, publications. This is satisfying hands-on imitation. But we must also strive to imitate the self-surrender of Jesus and his trust in the Father, summed up ultimately in Gethsemane ('Not my will but thine be done') or on Calvary ('Into thy hands I commend my spirit').

In making monastic vows we enter a lifestyle, tried and tested over centuries, that helps us enter into and participate in the self-surrender to and trust in God demonstrated by Jesus. In making vows in community we recognize our need for others to guide and encourage us, and we recognize as well our own limitations and weaknesses that can be helped and strengthened by others. In making vows we are choosing, and in living the vows we are constantly re-choosing God, as revealed through Christ: self-surrender and total self-giving love instead of a selfish and self-centred existence.

The discipline of the vows, often manifested in the corporate obligations of community life, habituates us in making our choice for God. Unfortunately, as with any opportunity afforded humans, disciplines can be used, misused and abused. The vowed life can be lived at a totally superficial level, though one hopes this does not happen. When old customs in community become divorced from the original purpose or meaning, we find ourselves as mere keepers of tradition rather than seekers of God. We must remain ever vigilant and discerning in our practices. What worked spiritually for an earlier generation, or assumptions that could be made even a generation ago, might be meaningless or inappropriate today. Here the new members can have a great impact on keeping a community viable. If the novices are asking why we do things a certain way, and our answers or explanations do not satisfy, then perhaps it is time for the community to ask itself the same questions. The answer can never be 'It's the tradition' or 'That's the way it's always been done'. If the outward expression of our vows no longer enables us to seek God and enter into his presence, if the discipline has become mechanical and empty – if the salt has lost its flavour! – then it should be discarded and replaced with a new discipline or expression that teaches today what the old disciplines taught yesterday. Vocations to the religious life are on the decline. Let us ask ourselves if it is because our lifestyle has lost its flavour?

Many communities are in the process of looking afresh at how they live their rule and vows. This can be both exciting and frightening, with each member having a slightly different proportional mix of anxiety and stimulation. Change stirs up any situation, and is more difficult for some than for others. Space must be made for members to grieve the passing of traditions, ministries and houses, as well as space made for the eagerness of those wanting to embrace the new and different. And then there is everyone in-between! That is community, and holding it together is a real living out of love. We are vowed to seek God in and through community, vowed to relationship with God and with community and with ourself (sometimes the most difficult relationship of all). Any viable relationship requires effort and change, compromise and sacrifice as it matures. The vowed life is the tilled soil in which we can grow, the daily life the tilling.

Perhaps in exploring the vowed life at a new millennium we need not to go back to our roots, which may be grounded in works or institutions, but to the vision which is in Christ, in Love Incarnated.

Mystery is being revealed, and revelation implies discovery. So we are not just on a journey, we are out to find Someone. The vowed life is a 'daring adventure'. We do not seek community for protection or security; it is not a form of 'sheltered accommodation' [3] for the pious. Communities of men and women under religious vows should be full of life – his life – places of mutual encouragement and places 'to grasp the breadth and length, the height and the depth, so that knowing the love of Christ, which is beyond knowledge, you may be filled with the fullness of God.' (Eph 3:18)

3. The phrases 'daring adventure' and 'sheltered accomodation' are from Alan Harrison's
    Bound for Life, Mowbray, London, 1983, p. 12.

SEVEN

'Though It Be Night'

GILLIAN RUTH CSMV

'Religious find themselves in a "Dark Night". The painful and intense moments of disintegration, which carry the hope for what can break through, characterize our living in this in-between.'[1] This description of the experience of members of American Roman Catholic religious orders applies equally to U.K. Anglican communities, as does Constance FitzGerald's concept of 'impasse' as a component of the dark night: 'By impasse I mean that there is no way out of, no way around, no rational escape from, what imprisons one, no possibilities in the situation.'[2] More recently, Sandra Schneiders has written of 'the apparent similarity between the character of the suffering that seems so widespread among Religious today and the nature of the Dark Night as it is described in John of the Cross … '[3]

In the context of religious life, the darkness and sense of impasse is expressed in the vicious circle of declining numbers and failure of the way of life to appeal in a pluralist, post-modern society. Former structures, value systems and ways of expressing religious commitment are no longer attractive or even relevant, and the darkness of the night has at its heart a sense of meaninglessness, from which there seems no possible way out.

Whilst Anglican religious life shares with Roman Catholic orders the discouragement evoked by decreasing numbers and decline in

1. 'Reflections upon the Religious Life of U.S. Women Religious.' Quoted in Elizabeth A. Johnson, 'Between the Times: Religious Life and the Post-modern Experience of God.' *Review for Religious* 53 (1994), p. 23.
2. Constance FitzGerald, 'Impasse and Dark Night.' In J. W. Conn, ed., *Women's Spirituality: Resources for Christian Development*, second edition. Paulist Press, New York, 1996, p. 410.
3. Sandra Schneiders, *Finding the Treasure: Locating Catholic Religious Life in a New Ecclesial and Cultural Context* [Religious Life in a New Millennium, Vol. 1.] Paulist Press, New York, 2000, p. 158.

'status', loss of identity and ultimate loss of meaning, this naming of the pain as a necessary step in its transformation has a distinct focus for Anglican communities. The revival of religious life in the Anglican Church in the mid-nineteenth century was rooted theologically in the Tractarian movement, and economically and politically in the industrial revolution, which created the educational and social needs of those who migrated to the cities. In the eyes of the Church, and of society generally, service, and not spirituality, was what justified the foundation of communities, and they became identified with great institutions. In the 1960s, the Community of St Mary the Virgin, Wantage, still ran schools in South Africa, India and England, as well as homes for unmarried mothers and their babies, residential centres for the care of the elderly, and an establishment for the rehabilitation of alcoholics and drug addicts. For this community, as for others, withdrawal from these works through lack of human resources and legislation regulating professional standards, signifies a loss of the identity bound up with the shared objectives of the work. The loss of what has, in the past, most given support leads to the erosion of all sense of security. It is precisely this loss of what gives security and support which characterises the experience which religious life is undergoing.

The metaphor of dark night used by the sixteenth century Spanish mystic John of the Cross describes a universal human experience. Dark night is only one of the Carmelite expressions of this, and Teresa of Avila talks about a similar experience in different imagery. There are clear parallels between what John and Teresa are describing, and the painful disorientation of contemporary religious, so that John of the Cross' metaphor of dark night, and Teresa of Avila's description of comparable experience, provide a framework within which to interpret this contemporary situation. The naming and owning of the dreadful darkness is an authentic expression of the death and rebirth which lie at the heart of the Gospel of Christ. The way through the pain is not to try to negotiate it by rationalisation, but to dare to live it as an open-ended engagement with God, in the darkness of faith, as a radical alternative to clinging to the structures and assumptions which block the bursting forth of new life.

John and Teresa were essentially writing for individuals, albeit individuals of whom many, though not all, were living in monastic communities. Consequently, there are passages in which John and Teresa talk specifically of the experience of personal prayer. Prayer is a lens which focuses the whole of life, and John and Teresa's concern with human life in its entirety enables their experience and spirituality to nourish and inform not only individuals, but communities and groups who are committed to journeying together with a shared vision. It is with this in mind that we examine the experience reported by John of the Cross and Teresa of Avila, using the Carmelite texts to try to bring new meaning to a situation in which many Anglican religious find themselves at present. For many aspects of this experience, 'dark night' is a startlingly apt metaphor.

CHANGE IN THE EXPERIENCE OF GOD

Undergirding the destabilisation and disorientation for which dark night is the appropriate analogy is a change in the experience of God. John of the Cross delineates the Christian journey as a movement from love and desire suffused with self-interest and possessiveness and the accompanying lack of freedom, to a purified love which is centred on God and is the focused energy of an integrated person. It is within this very night of stripping and purification that the process of transformation is taking place.

Each religious community has its sense of corporate vocation and ethos which has emerged from the vision inspiring the initial stages of its foundation, before structures and particular modes of expression were defined. Once the tradition is more firmly established, the necessity of protecting established expressions from whatever threatens them curtails the flexibility of the earlier vision. That very vision, grounded in love of God and desire to serve him in others, has now to be laid before that purifying love so that it can be changed and adapted to its contemporary context. The necessary surrender of what has supported, inspired and energised, but now stifles life, feels like the death of all meaning. The rediscovery of meaning requires a new synthesis of vision and context. If this synthesis does not emerge, the eventual result will be termination. Only if there is willing engagement in this process will the new experience of God be one of spirit-kindled fire.

What the metaphor of the 'dark night' describes, then, is the conflicts engendered by that stripping of the egotistical self which acts as a barrier between human beings and the God of love. 'Appropriately, this constricted road is called a dark night,'[4] John writes, letting the image itself speak powerfully for him. Although Teresa does not use the same term, there is much in her writing, principally in the text of *The Interior Castle,* which may be identified with the experience John is describing in *The Ascent of Mount Carmel* and *The Dark Night.*

THE DARK NIGHT IN JOHN OF THE CROSS

The two treatises by John of the Cross, written in 1581-85, and 1584-85 respectively, were intended as commentaries on his poem *The Dark Night,* written earlier, in 1578 or 1579, and vividly recalling his escape from the traumas of his imprisonment in Toledo. Near the beginning of Book II of *The Ascent,* however, John abandoned his commentary on the poem at the second of the eight stanzas and gave his full attention to describing the active night of spirit. In John's scheme, the night is active when the person is willingly surrendering to it with some degree of initiative, and passive where there is no sense of control, but a conviction that the work is being effected by God. There has nevertheless to be continuing openness to what is happening. John also distinguishes between sense and spirit, the external and affective as distinct from what is inward and integrated. *The Dark Night* explores the passive night of sense and spirit by means of a commentary on the first three stanzas of the poem. It is his poetry

4. *The Collected Works of St John of the Cross*, trans. by K. Kavanaugh and O. Rodriguez, revised edition, Institute of Carmelite Studies, Washington, 1991. 'The Dark Night' (DN), Prologue.

which expresses the depths of John's prayer, and whilst his prose writing synthesizes the spiritual life with support from both biblical sources and scholastic theology, the interweaving of his poetry with his prose communicates the dimension of vibrant experience.

THE FIRST PART OF THE NIGHT

John's metaphor divides the night into three parts, like natural night. 'The first part, the night of the senses,' John explains, 'resembles early evening, that time of twilight when things begin to fade from sight.'[5] Those who desire God must cease to be dominated by the appetites and cravings of the physical senses, the imagination and the emotions. 'When the appetites are extinguished – or mortified – one no longer feeds on the pleasure of these things, but lives in a void and in darkness with respect to the appetites.'[6] Although the active aspects of the dark night begin to plunge the person who desires God into a painful void, the asceticism of denial of the senses advocated by John always leaves room for a residue of control, a sense of spiritual achievement in which the ego dominates. 'The ascetical self,' Turner writes, 'is the best we can hope to achieve by way of our own, albeit grace-assisted efforts: a more or less well-adjusted arrangement of the forces of an elemental egoism.'[7]

The discipline and privilege of the daily Eucharist, the Divine Office and personal prayer, balanced by active service, have been the familiar contours of the life of Anglican religious since communities began to expand before the end of the nineteenth century. Whilst religious enjoyed a certain self-confidence derived from success and status, they also showed generosity and dedication in prayer and ministry and a readiness to respond to the call of God to demanding enterprises, both in Britain and overseas – running schools, hospitals and other care establishments. Religious life drew out of sisters and brothers commitment, focus and a real self-denial. The offering they

5. *The Collected Works of St John of the Cross*, 'The Ascent of Mount Carmel' (Asc.) 1.2.5
6. Asc. I.3.1
7. Denys Turner, *The Darkness of God: Negativity in Christian Mysticism*, Cambridge University Press, Cambridge, 1995. p. 242.

made was rooted in meaning and enhanced the meaning of lives offered to God through the community.

The undermining of this sense of meaning in the context of the withdrawal from institutional works, precipitated by increasing state control of social services in the 1950s and 1960s, created disorientation and loss of identity. Such emptiness has a parallel expression in a prayer life which becomes dry and unsatisfying.

Correspondingly, John comments: 'Since the conduct of these beginners is lowly and not too distant from the love of pleasure and of self ... God desires to ... lead them on to a higher degree of divine love.' [8] One effect of this shift is a distinction between the nature of the person's previous prayer and its present character. John reports in both *The Ascent* and *The Dark Night* that discursive meditation becomes dry and distracted: 'Dryness is now the outcome of fixing the senses on subjects that formerly provided satisfaction.' [9] Instead, peaceful recollection occurs without the help of images: 'the soul, as one with a store of water, drinks peaceably without the labour and the need to fetch the water through the channels of past considerations, forms and figures.' [10] This can seem like sheer waste of time, and those who pray in this way sense regression in their relationship with God: 'the soul thinks it is not serving God but turning back, because it is aware of this distaste for the things of God.' [11]

THE SECOND PART OF THE NIGHT

Such apparent distaste for the things of God is, on the contrary, a result of greater receptivity to his imperceptible inflowing. The purification of the intellect, the memory and the will which John has described in Books II and III of *The Ascent* as the active night of spirit has already begun to deepen the person's receptivity to God. What is grasped by the intellect is replaced by the darkness of faith in what is not seen; what the memory retains is relinquished for hope in what is

8. DN I.8.3
9. Asc. II.13.2. See DN I.9.8
10. Asc, II.14.2
11. DN I.9.3. See I.10.5

not possessed, what the will controls is let go of for the utter givenness of love.

For contemporary religious, intellectual insight and clarity of religious belief have been challenged by post-modern secularism, on the one hand, and the call to inter-faith dialogue, on the other. Religious boundaries are no longer clear-cut, and we are left with the darkness of faith. The collapse of the stability and security previously built on community identity and tradition, demands hope in a future that is unknown. The erosion of hierarchical structures and the move away from unquestioning obedience evoke a deeper response to the call of love and require each individual to take responsibility for his or her personal choices and for the corporate life of the whole.

John goes on to describe the contemplative purgation of the passive night of the spirit. Commenting on the first stanza of the poem, 'One dark night … I went out unseen,'[12] he writes: 'I departed from my low manner of understanding, and my feeble way of loving, and my poor and limited method of finding satisfaction in God.'[13] The person's active engagement is preparation for the middle and darkest part of the night which has arrived. 'The second part, faith, is completely dark, like midnight.'[14] Edith Stein, contrasting the willingly entered night of the senses with the passive night of faith in terms of a voluntary carrying of the cross as against crucifixion, states that a person 'can surrender himself [sic] to crucifixion, but he cannot crucify himself Hence what has been begun in the active Night must be perfected by the passive Night, that is, by God himself.'[15]

In practice, this darkest part of the night is experienced most painfully in the spiritual heart of common life, the corporate prayer of the community. Although the accepted *raison d'etre* of Anglican foundations was work and service, most had from their beginnings a strong commitment to corporate prayer which, as numbers increased,

12. DN II.4
13. DN II.4.1
14. Asc. I.2.5
15. Edith Stein, *The Science of the Cross: A Study of St. John of the Cross*, trans. by H. Graef, Burns and Oates, London, 1960, p. 33.

developed into a full seven- or eightfold monastic Office, using plainsong in the Gregorian or similar traditions. Declining numbers and shifts in the balance of time have led in the past thirty years to an overall decrease in the number of daily Offices. Liturgical innovation, contemporary translation of the psalms and other Scripture and, perhaps most significantly, the need for the Office to nurture and not to impose a burden, has led many communities to revise and simplify their Office. Many members have welcomed this: for them, the darkness was experienced in the daily recitation of an Office which no longer entirely reflected contemporary life and spirituality. For others, changes to the Office are a deprivation of the familiar expression of the prayer which is at the centre of the consecrated life. When spiritual privileges are taken away, the night is at its darkest.

John compares the necessary purgation of all that blocks the person's response to God with the stage in the burning of a log of wood when 'by drying out the wood, the fire brings to light and expels all those ugly and dark accidents that are contrary to fire.'[16] It is a necessary process in the final transformation of the log of wood into the beauty of the fire itself.'[17] 'As the soul is purged and purified by this fire of love, it is further enkindled in love … '[18] Love of God and desire for God sustain the person throughout the painful process of purification. Those who love are willing for God to deconstruct the way in which they love God, and still to continue loving him.

TERESA OF AVILA'S EXPERIENCE OF DISORIENTATION

For Teresa also, the beginning and end of her experience is love, and as we move on to draw out threads in her writing which resonate with what John says about the dark night, we hold all that she has to say in the context of her desire for God. 'The important thing is not to think much but to love much,'[19] she famously remarks. The comment is made at the point at which Teresa, describing a change which occurs

16. DN II.10.1
17. Ibid.
18. DN II.10.6
19. *The Collected Works of St. Teresa of Avila*, Vol. 2. Institute of Carmelite Studies, Washington, 1980. 'The Interior Castle' (Int. C.) IV.1.7.

in a person's way of praying, distinguishes between 'consolations' and ' spiritual delights' . In her description of consolations in the first chapter of the fourth dwelling place, there is an echo of the gratification which can be earned from participation in the active night of sense described by John – an awareness of human wellbeing

Teresa uses the image of the two water-troughs to convey what she means by prayer which results in spiritual delight.[20] The effort involved in discursive meditation is depicted by water being channelled through aqueducts. Delight is given when God acts with greater freedom in the soul, producing interior peace and stillness from the soul's depths, like water welling up from a spring. For Teresa, the resulting happiness is different from that arising from an exterior, more 'worldly' source. She now highlights the problem that, in this new focus of the soul, distractions can appear to be worse because the intellect, caught up in God, is no longer able to process the flow of thought, and the imagination wanders without restraint. Even further on, in the sixth dwelling place, Teresa argues for the continued use of discursive meditation to help with this problem: 'My soul, it seems to me, was like a bird flying about that doesn't know where to light.' [21]

As with John's dark night experience, prayer produces an increased interiority which throws inner brokenness, normally kept in equilibrium by the conscious mind's absorption in activity, into sharpened clarity. Rowan Williams offers this description of what is going on: 'bits and pieces of desire and fantasy, vanity, lust, resentment ... will come much more clearly into conscious focus when the understanding, at its deepest level, faces the divine reality that it cannot conceptualize.'[22]

As in John's account of this transitional stage, struggle combines with peaceful awareness of God's presence. Only in the later dwelling places does Teresa describe the real suffering which accompanies growth, and for this she uses the powerful metaphor of the silkworm/

20. Int. C. IV.2.3
21. Int. C. VI.7. 15
22. Rowan Williams, *Teresa of Avila* [Outstanding Christian Thinkers] Geoffrey Chapman, London, 1991. p. 124.

butterfly, an image both of the pain, and of the healing and new life in God which are at the heart of what is happening.

In spite of the fact that nowhere does Teresa call this experience a 'dark night', there are obvious common threads in John's account of the passive nights and Teresa's description of the butterfly spinning itself a cocoon. Her confusion of moths and butterflies [23] takes nothing away from the vividness of her analogy between the interior move-ment towards God described in the Fourth, Fifth and Sixth Dwelling Places, and the dark death of the silkworm in its cocoon: 'Let this silkworm die, as it does in completing what it was created to do! And you will see how we see God, as well as ourselves placed inside His greatness, as is this little silkworm within its cocoon.' [24] Within the cocoon of God's greatness, the total disintegration of the silkworm is necessary in order for it to emerge transformed as a butterfly. There is a total breakdown of the creature's composition, and a total remaking, in which the silkworm has become a passive participant.

Teresa makes a contrast between the stage where 'we ourselves put the silkworm to death' [25] and the state where 'in the delightful union, the experience of seeing oneself in so new a life greatly helps one to die.' [26] By 'the delightful union' she is referring to infused contempla-tion. Teresa's analogy is comparable with John's distinction between the active and passive nights, between stripping of the self willingly and actively undertaken and a purification in which the person is helpless. In the Sixth Dwelling Place, Teresa goes on to describe the intense suffering in which the trustworthiness of God at the centre of the castle is doubted: 'The Lord, it seems, gives the devil licence so that the soul might be tried and even made to think it is rejected by God … I don't know what to compare this experience to if not the oppression of those that suffer in hell … ' [27] The soul also begins to feel that it has turned away from God: 'The soul doesn't think that it has

23. See John Welch, *Spiritual Pilgrims: Carl Jung and Teresa of Avila*, Paulist Press, New York, 1982, p. 138.
24. Int. C. V.2.6
25. Int. C. V.3.5
26. Ibid.
27. Int. C. VI. 1.9

any love of God or that it ever had any … ' [28]

Teresa's description of the effect of this suffering has clear parallels to the dark night described by John of the Cross. Both report emptiness and disorientation. There is a radical loss of security as the person moves into the unknown, and the lack of familiar structures undermines the sense of identity. Using her metaphor of the journey to the centre of the interior castle, Teresa reflects in her conversational style, with frequent digressions, the experience which John expresses in systematic form. The intellect fails to construct meaning, which is rediscovered in faith; the memory's task of creating identity is dispossessed and found in hope; the will's control is lost, to be transformed in love. John states that this way of negation applies both to the sensory and the spiritual dimensions of human beings, and cites his celebrated verses in this connection:

> To come to the knowledge of all
> desire the knowledge of nothing …
> To come to be what you are not
> you must go by a way in which you are not.[29]

If this dark night is to be transformed into the light of a closer union with God, it is crucial that the soul's desire and love continue to undergird the experience. The soul will thus be willing to wait with longing, hope and faith as a context in which powerlessness, meaninglessness and fear can be sustained. This is possible only if the pain is fully recognised and named, and the desirability of the darkness as necessary for growth in union with God is acknowledged. John's metaphor of purified desire is the flame of the Holy Spirit in the very centre of the soul. 'The soul feels him within itself not only as a fire that has consumed and transformed it but as a fire that burns and flares up within it.' [30] Teresa describes the soul's transformation as 'a little white butterfly [which] comes forth.' [31] Each is describing the transforma-

28. Int. C. VI.l.11
29. Asc. I.13.11
30. *The Collected Works of St John of the Cross*, 'The Living Flame of Love' (LF) 1.3

tion of desire from its humanly ambiguous and possessive nature to what is integrated and whole.

THE PURIFICATION OF DESIRE FOR GOD

In a brilliant synthesis of the factors in religious awareness influencing both atheism and contemplation, Michael Buckley asserts the human tendency to delineate a God who is a projection of personal needs and desires. This view of religious consciousness, Buckley argues, corresponds with the warning from John of the Cross that we love and desire a God of our own making.

What Buckley is asserting is affirmed by what we find in the texts. On the line, 'fired with love's urgent longings', John comments: 'A love of pleasure, and attachment to it, usually fires the will toward the enjoyment of things that give pleasure. A more intense enkindling of another, better love (love of the soul's Bridegroom) is necessary for the vanquishing of the appetites and the denial of this pleasure.' [32] Buckley describes this ongoing purification of the soul's engagement with God as 'a progressive hermeneutic of the nature of God,' [33] made possible by 'the progressive purification and transformation of the person through what he [sic] cherishes and through what gives him security and support.' [34]

THE CHALLENGE TO ENTER THE DARKNESS

Religious orders faced with the loss of what supports and gives security cannot hope to come through the darkness without first naming the confusion surrounding the shifts in belief systems and values, the loss of identity previously found in major institutional works, and the pain and grief which all this entails. We are invited to enter the night, to welcome it and the shift it involves in our relationship with God, and so to discover in new ways the shared vision and the common life which are at the heart of religious life. The dark night

31. Int. C. V.2.7
32. Asc. I.14.2
33. M. J. Buckley, 'Atheism and Contemplation', *Theological Studies* 40 (1979) p. 696.
34. Ibid.

in its corporate dimension needs the assent of each member to engage with the darkness. It calls for each to be willing to acceptance change in the ways they experience God. If some are unable to walk in the dark, or refuse to accept the darkness, commitment to the night ceases to be corporate and the result is fragmentation. Ongoing dialogue, openness with each other, and readiness to listen to others' opinions, hopes, reservations and fears, are essential as a constant counterbalance to the possibility of fragmentation.

This naming, welcoming and engaging in dialogue have, above all to be earthed in the context of daily life. Community life, in its daily encounters, prevents sisters and brothers from becoming exclusively preoccupied with their individual journeys. The rebirth of meaning through the renewal of identity, individual and corporate, which is founded on Christ, begins where the person and the community is, in the reality of the material world. It is here that we are to welcome the night into which we have been invited, appropriating it into the context of everyday living. Here, religious communities discover what Mary Grey terms 'the inter-connectedness of divine and human becoming'.[35] Writing of the dark night in the experience of women, her encouragement applies equally to religious communities: 'Although there is no comfort and even no real hope experienced for the future, and memories of the past bring no security, the process demands that we move forward ... trust in the absent God our guide – to an alternative we have no name for, only yearning.'[36]

THE THIRD PART OF JOHN OF THE CROSS'S NIGHT

Out of the emptiness which lovingly draws us to surrender our own images of God, new vision is born. The painful journey through the first two phases of John's night – the gathering darkness and the pitch dark – has brought us to the third part of the night,[37] the threshold of dawn, where the light of God is glimpsed. It is a light in whose

35. Mary Grey, *Redeeming the Dream: Feminism. Redemption and Christian Tradition*, SPCK, London, 1989, p. 80.
36. Ibid.
37. Asc. I.2.5

brightness religious perceive the fragility of past securities: reputable and effective institutional works; the strength of numbers; the habit as a symbol carrying universal meaning; status and the respect of the Church and of those who neither claim nor wish for affiliation to it. These things were good and appropriate in their context and time, just as, in the writing of John of the Cross, the devout life, asceticism and discursive prayer of the person striving to follow Christ were commendable. The journey through the night has stripped away meaning and security and engendered a greater detachment which brings vulnerability.

The spirituality of the first Anglican sisters was, above all, one which embraced this vulnerability. They had abandoned the security of family life protected by father or husband for a life lived among other women who, albeit under the protection of a bishop or other clerical male, were not readily accepted by Church or society, and whose future was totally uncertain. It may be that what religious are being called to recognise through the dark and painful emptiness is that God is calling them to an identity which is deeper than one based on institutional success; and that such an identity finds itself in vulnerability. Relinquishing the old identity engenders a vulnerability which can only be sustained where Christ's resurrection is lived out at the heart of the material world.

A heightened awareness of vulnerability has come about through living the common life in smaller groups. Such a lifestyle requires openness with each other and commitment to a shared vision within whose contours each member's ministry is owned by all. In the absence of the bonds created by institutional works, the gradual evolution of such a vision resembles Teresa's butterfly emerging from its cocoon, struggling and fragile, yet full of creative potential. Total openness to and dependence on the movement of the Spirit precludes reliance on social and material security. A number of communities have earthed this aspect of their common life by living in poorer areas where bonds with society's most vulnerable people can be formed and the community itself ne enriched and informed by their nearness.

Anglican religious are invited to welcome the dark night as an expression of the vulnerability of being human, experiencing loss, death and rebirth as part of the mystery of life. Recognition of the darkness for what it is, and commitment to it for the love of God, are essential parts of the process. John of the Cross, drawn by desire for the Beloved, went out 'with no other light or guide / than the one that burned in my heart.' [38]

---

38. DN II.25 (third stanza).

EIGHT

Developing Religious Identity

ALISTAIR SSF

'The kingdom of heaven is like a mustard seed that someone took and sowed in his field; it is the smallest of all the seeds, but when it has grown it is the greatest of shrubs and becomes a tree, so that the birds of the air come and make nests in its branches.' (Mt 13:31-32)

WHAT ARE WE SUPPOSED TO BE?

The habit as identity

The story is told in our community of a brother, renowned for his use of the *bon mot,* who, one day travelling in the London Underground and dressed in our Franciscan habit, was confronted and questioned by an unspecified clergyman: 'What are you supposed to be?' 'I'm supposed to be polite,' the brother answered, 'what are you supposed to be?'

To what extent the questioner was satisfied with this answer is not recorded. However, the exchange does serve well my purpose of being alert, from the outset of this essay on religious identity, to a distinction between what in the popular imagination we, as religious, are supposed to be and what, or who, in truth, we are and might become. Moreover, I confess that I did not appreciate this distinction between identifying with the *role* of a religious and being in a proper relationship with that particular identity when I was first clothed as a novice in my community some twenty years ago.

After the clothing, the first thing I did when I was alone was to think where I could possibly find a full-length mirror. Sensibly, religious houses are a bit short on mirrors. The only place to find a decent one is in the sacristy where the priests vest for Mass. Yet, it did not really matter. I could practise taking my habit off and putting it on again (and again) in the sure knowledge of what I had now become, and that this is what I was supposed to be.

The religious as archetype, role, icon

Doubtless, religious have experienced many different thoughts and feelings when they have first donned their habits – including 'this is a ghastly mistake'. Nevertheless, inevitably, there are common elements in the experience of all which can be drawn from the above. 'Inevitable' because the image of a habited monk or nun or friar or sister presents so powerfully the role or icon of some sort of 'holy man' or 'holy woman' in our culture. A Jungian would talk of this image as reflecting an archetype from the collective unconscious. More prosaically, one might say that, regardless of one's knowledge of Christianity or any religion, as one grows up, one cannot fail to learn and absorb some 'meaning' of the habit, alongside the meaning of the other myriad of images permeating our culture; images which immediately inform us about a person's role: policeman, nurse, white-coated scientist, judge, soldier, prostitute, social worker, mother, vicar.

When we have friends who are employed in some of these particular professions we know that within the role there is a real person more like ourselves than the image. However, when we meet a 'uniform', of whatever sort, our immediate response is to react to the role rather than to a person like ourselves. In the complex social order of our culture, where people have specialised tasks and professions, this makes sense. Other people are potentially the most unpredictable and uncontrollable elements in our environment. For the smooth running of society we all need to know what to expect from other people when we meet them in their different roles. We need to know how to elicit from them the responses we want and to be able to anticipate what they are going to do.

Importantly, the proper playing out of the rules of a particular role is not only the responsibility of the 'uniform'. Rather, for the role to function as it should, it needs to be complemented by the other playing the reciprocal role: patient to nurse, pupil to teacher, law-abiding citizen to policeman, parish priest to bishop. Indeed, as we grow up, we never learn simply an isolated role but always a pair of reciprocal roles; and in situations where there is either a conspicuous asymmetry of power within the relationship or an uncertainty in how we should behave, there is a strong social pressure to conform to the expectations of these reciprocal roles.[1]

When I put on my new habit, I already knew, without having to be taught it, what I was supposed to be and how I was supposed to behave and relate to others in the world. I also knew how they should perceive and behave towards me: as different, unknown, other, special, admirable in some way. And I knew of the strong social expectations that would not only recruit us into our reciprocal roles but also keep us in this particular holy dance around the habit, around a caricature of the religious life.

When I say I 'knew', it didn't mean that this was a self-reflective, self-conscious knowledge: rather the role inhabited me and I simply took it for granted that I had become that person. I (over)-identified with the role, and the world colluded with me and pressurised me into acting it out. We were both equally ignorant of what the religious life might really be about.

In the popular imagination the religious life stands for a whole cluster of characteristics: a single-sex institutional life, individual (if not corporate) poverty, celibacy, being obedient to your superiors within an ordered hierarchy, a prescribed lifestyle with no choices to make, a life of prayer and service to others. As a cultural stereotype the religious should be spiritual, poor, powerless, asexual, simple, good, loving, other-worldly, completely self-giving, innocent, harmless, quaint. As such, he or she is not really understood but can be admired and revered. Real religious should be like this, and the world

---

1. The term 'reciprocal-role', used to denote the clustering of a particular set of 'procedures' by which a relationship may be temporally organised, derives from the work of the British psychotherapist Dr Anthony Ryle. The concept represents a modification of some ideas from within Object Relations Theory. For further reading see, for example, A. Ryle (Ed.), *Cognitive Analytic Therapy – Developments in Theory and Practice*, John Wiley & Sons, Chichester, 1995.

tolerates little deviation from this list of attributes; otherwise, at best, religious may be seen as irrelevant, making an escape from the real world, or at worst sinister, sexually perverse, parasites on society.

Ideals and dangers

Of course, I was young and psychologically immature when I was first clothed in the habit. It is easy to look back with a wry smile as I reflect on that early identification with a stereotype. Many other men and women today test their vocation later in life when one imagines their personalities are more formed and mature; and the extent to which religious wear the habit varies from community to community. Also, in fairness to myself and most novices, at the time, I believed that I was called to the religious life and, sincerely, I wished to sacrifice my life in prayer and in the service of others with an unconditional Christ-like love. The image of the habit authentically focused these ideals, and sharing in the companionship of a religious community seemed the natural context in which to pursue them.

Yet, because the habit is such a powerful symbol, it is potentially dangerous as well as creative. If we insist on wearing the habit – and I think we should – we can expect to experience the pressure of the world (and that pressure internalised in our own psyche making the same demand upon ourselves) insisting that we live out a stereotype of the religious life. The great danger for us is if we fail to uncouple from the romance, the encapsulated ideal of the religious. For, however attractive and admirable the archetype of the religious, the habit is a shell, an empty shell which threatens to trap and suffocate us in a dying relationship with the world and with Christ if we allow this to become our only source of identity. Without a growth in psychological maturity and the development of understanding of an intimacy of real relationship, the vacuum may be filled by acting out the pattern of religious life in order to meet the expectations of the world. To over-identify with the archetype of the religious would ultimately be spiritual death.

The 'habit': one identity one relationship among many

In deliberately using the 'habit' as a metaphor for all initial expectations of the identity of religious, I have sought to be alert to the danger of identification with this symbol. Instead, we need to find a proper relationship with the 'habit'. Religious identity is not identification with one static icon or ideal. Rather, it is the process, from within a particular context, of learning true relationship through multiple engagements with the world, but equally in particular relationships, in my relationship with my community and, fundamentally, in my relationship of dying and rising with Christ.

When I first donned the habit, the identification with this stereotype or archetype seemed like a satisfying arrival into a life, I think of it now as merely a point – albeit a necessary point – of departure on a long journey towards true life.

COMMUNITY AS IDENTITY

Acknowledging non-theological discourses

We are often asked: 'Why did you join the religious life?' We know that an equally good, if not better, question is: 'Why did you stay? Answering in the language of 'vocation', 'grace', 'devotion', 'sacrifice' and 'service' is, I believe, valid.

But equally valid and necessary are psychological, sociological and economic accounts which together can give a more complete explanation. These analyses from within other discourses are helpful both in undercutting an overly naive and comfortable resting in the romantic religious identity, and in that they challenge us to articulate our more valuable message and true identity to a secular world. Also, experience shows, living within a community of the religious life is (and should be) a long exercise in coming to know oneself and honestly facing these often unexpected truths from other discourses.

Entering community – new and old identities

The crucible of community life needs to be a psychologically safe place for this process of self-discovery to proceed. Becoming a member of a religious order should not be like joining an organisation. Rather one is entering into a relationship with one's community, with all the twists and turns that an ongoing and deepening relationship over a life-time implies. One's identity is inevitably shaped by this process, for the relationships we inhabit forge our identities. The conception of relationship (and identity) as reciprocal-role-play in the 'world', as discussed above, is of equal value for describing the dynamics of some interpersonal relationships within this different domain of the 'community'.

Although one may know intuitively how a habited religious ought to relate to the world (and the world to it) a whole new more subtle set of expectations of how one should behave towards others within the community needs to be learned. One enters a novel subculture with its own particular customs, rules and hierarchies regulating the functions of the group. As with all groups, while some of these expectations are written down, much is not always consciously articulated; indeed, one of the most important things to learn is often the distinction between what is said and what (as most everyone in the group understands) actually happens.

However socially-skilled and confident one may have been in the world, one is immediately deskilled within this new social environment: a novice with little status and, in terms of one's present and future life, seemingly quite dependent upon one's superiors. (When one becomes a superior, however, novices seem anything but dependent, powerless or helpless !) In this situation of social uncertainty, living very closely with others in asymmetric power relationships, the dynamics of early parent-child reciprocal-roles are inevitably called forth.

Also, for many of us called by the siren of the promise of a perfect, ideal identity as a religious, this vocation represented, in part at least, a psychological need to make good, by this substitution, major deficiencies in the identity we felt we already possessed. But within a healthy community, thankfully, such 'perfection' is not easily tolerated – it just does not feel quite human enough. Without one's brothers and sisters offering the required constant admiration, this particular reciprocal-role is not fed, it shrivels, and one soon falls back to one's former reciprocal-roles, often, particularly, those one had hoped most to expunge from one's personality and consign to the dustbin of one's former identity.

Parent-child relationships

It's a fairly good bet that if one emerged into adulthood with the feeling (or worse still, *not* knowing the feeling) that one somehow is not good enough, then one's early history, perhaps one's experience of being parented, somehow contrived to impair one's basic sense of self-esteem, compromising the basis of one's identity. Whatever unresolved emotional legacy one brings into the religious life, the traditional structures and practices of many communities can provide a rich context in which such unhelpful reciprocal-roles can flourish.

In joining a religious community it can feel that one is stripped of all the responsibilities and decision-making that are part and parcel of being an adult: earning a living, finding somewhere to live, choosing with whom you live and the lifestyle you wish and can afford to pursue. The traditional image of a religious order as a rigid hierarchy, built on a plethora of rules and unquestioning obedience – a disciplined 'ground-force' for God, or a powerhouse of prayer – may have forged some sort of necessary heroic identity in the past. But in today's world, properly, we see this mixture of uncertain psychological maturity and close interpersonal engagement within the context of asymmetric, dependent power relationships in an enclosed world of community as potentially disastrous for the formation of a healthy identity.

The formal rules and principles of religious community, however, testify to the wisdom of our founders who grasped intuitively the need to foster something we might now call psychological maturity. Nevertheless, it would be foolish to think that we can altogether avoid the more subtle acting out of the ways of relating we have learnt from our former lives just because we've entered a religious community. For our identities to be reformed, we must first of all see ourselves acting them out, but in an environment which does not collude with our attempts to recruit a particular sort of parent to our particular child. Wise, psychologically astute novice-guardians, chapters and superiors can offer an experience of good reparative parenting to lead us towards psychological adulthood: parenting which engenders unconditionally a genuine dialogue of attentiveness to, and respect for, what the other has to say. This process of growth into psychological adulthood is uneven and slow. It is questionable if anyone ever achieves it completely, and the mark of being an adult is maybe to know that one has not yet reached it.

The beginning of self-knowledge:
group dynamics and corporate identity
Alongside parent-child roles, each brings to community ways in which one has learnt to relate to one's peers.

We are all familiar with finding ourselves behaving in subtly different ways with different individuals and in different situations. It is unpleasant to find that on occasion our identity seems also to include a number of less admirable reciprocal-roles – hurtful critic to injured criticised; self-righteous prig to sinner; overbearing control freak to resentful/compliant/ controlled; contemptuous to contemptible; bully to victim. We can induce these patterns of relating and play these roles from either pole; and once we become caught-up in such exchanges, it is easy to become locked into these damaging relationships.

Group interactions seem especially to constellate such dynamics in unpredictable and virulent ways. In the enclosed systems of the contemplative life, such bitternesses can persist for years. Also, in more active communities, where the personnel in a group change more frequently, it can be quite unsettling to see how the power of the group dynamic can change with the absence or arrival of a brother or sister. Subtle power struggles shift their focus, loyalties change, new alliances within the group are formed and suddenly one may be acting out a new role within the group. Such is the pressure of group dynamics that this can be very difficult to resist and change; there is a group identity which is greater than the sum of its parts.

This is a mixed blessing. On the one hand, there may be a security and satisfaction in finding a valued niche or role within the group; but, on the other hand, one may feel pushed into a role which is less positive and uncomfortable. On both counts the role conferred by the group threatens one's individual autonomy and the development of a psychologically more rich and mature identity.

Another distinction is between an identity which is given as a particular role within the group and an identification with the group as a whole. The corporate strength of the group identity is most often invoked when the community as a whole is threatened or damaged either from without by the world or from within by loss: through death, expulsion or someone choosing to leave. Under threat, the collective identity can polarise all across a firm boundary of one being either *inside* or *outside* the group. However close one may have been to a particular brother or sister, if they choose to leave the community one's relationship changes even though both parties may hope that it will not.

Psychological maturity and intimacy

Growth towards psychological maturity must go hand in hand with our needs for close loving relationships and our efforts to love others. Most people who join the religious life leave it. For some of these individuals who leave, their experience of community living has served them well in terms of what they have learned about themselves and their particular needs; and they have learned that their journey must continue outside the religious life. Others, perhaps, despite their community's well-intentioned efforts, leave because the religious life has not served them well in the furtherance of their Christian vocation. Religious communities can 'fail' their members either when they cannot provide the particular sort of opportunities for psychological growth that some require, or, in terms of interpersonal relationships, the community has not fostered a rewarding intimacy between its members. When a religious order facilitates psychological maturity but neglects to foster emotional interdependence among its members, it increasingly becomes an 'organisation' rather than a 'community'.

Those who stay, however, do so because, much of the time, it is enjoyable. The picture of a continuously dysfunctional therapeutic community given above is a harsh analysis and cannot simply do justice to the seriousness of our project as religious. It is by the grace of God that we have been called into the religious life. Our vocation is too important a privilege to put a 'holy spin' on the realities of our lives and side-step our all-too-human frailties and failings. For it is only in the humility of acknowledging the truth about ourselves that we turn to Christ, and can take the first steps towards engaging in true relationship with our brothers and sisters, with our community and with the world.

DIALOGUE AND SELF-REFLECTION

Change within particular relationships

A suggestion throughout this essay is that our identities reside within the various patterns of relationship we inhabit. Our attention has been drawn to some relationships which may especially go towards forming a religious identity. Not all religious identities have been discussed – our relationship with the institution of the Church, for some, with priesthood, with our founders (e.g. an identity as a Franciscan or a Benedictine), with religious of other communities – and, of course, each of us enjoys other relationships in our lives which may not have any obvious religious dimension. Our conclusion might therefore be that in having multiple relationships we have multiple identities.

Yet for most of us, it feels as if the same familiar 'I' has a substantial continuity across 'my' various relationships. I behave fairly predictably, though differently, in different social situations, in the patterns of relationship which I establish, the qualitative characteristics of the way in which I relate show consistency: I have *an* identity. Yet an objective observer would surprise most of us if he told us some of the truth about ourselves.

But being *told* the truth, and *hearing* the truth about ourselves and then changing, are two quite different things. The power of group pressure may force or coerce us to listen, oblige us to comply, but under most circumstances community dynamics do not in themselves promote the sort of individual self-reflection that allows us easily to acknowledge (let alone know how to change) the disparity between the life we espouse and our hidden motives and self-deceptions. Such honesty and change happens – perhaps only happens – within the intimacy of particular relationships when one knows that one is loved.

This statement needs to be qualified, yet without robbing the words 'intimacy' and 'love' of their immediacy and the sense of a living encounter which they are intended to evoke. The key qualification is 'loved in the power of the Spirit'. In introducing into a largely psychological account an explicit reference to God, some thought on the relationship between the psychological and the theological is now necessary. Indeed, this is central to a discussion on the essence of religious identity as residing within relationship. Clearly, our priority as Christians in the religious life is to find expression of that identity within a Christian theological discourse. A purely psychological account of ourselves is inadequate.

Psychological and theological understandings

Psychological models are essentially provisional theories to be discussed, and debated, and eventually discarded, to be replaced by better humanly-generated theories. Psychological discourse may be powerful and persuasive in suggesting understandings of human behaviour and experience, both private and, more especially, within human relationships. But its provisional psychological treatment of the human spirit must not be confused with the truth to which the theological discourse seeks to point regarding God's revelation of his relationship to humanity, through Jesus Christ, in the power of the Holy Spirit. The theological has priority over all other discourses. In as much as I know these revealed truths, I know them through faith. They are not up for discussion in the same way as psychological constructs; they may be further explored and reinterpreted but, in some essential way, they are non-negotiable. Rather, through grace, I assert and proclaim this faith in revelation.

Psychological understandings and theological understandings must not be confused, and Christians will give the priority to revealed theological truths. They are two completely different discourses. But, in practice, what the psychological and the theological address, respectively, the *psyche* (and the *soma*) and the action or power of the Holy Spirit – are, experientially, inseparable.

I've got only one brain, one set of experiences, events, desires, and relationships with others and the world of which to make sense and to interpret. Moreover, anyone, Christian or otherwise, in being human, simply can not avoid engaging in psychological thinking. We all employ some 'theory of mind' – implicit psychological models of intra- and interpersonal experience – to make sense of our own day-to-day experience and to predict the behaviour of others. Indeed, the immense complexity of human beings makes it an absolute necessity.

The suggestion that the psychological treatment of the human spirit and the theological workings of the Holy Spirit cannot be separated but neither, since one is a human understanding and the other of God, must they be confused, is, perhaps, contentious. In defence of this 'formula', however, attention might be drawn to the Council of Chalcedon (A.D. 451). In addressing the christological controversies of how the Church should understand Jesus Christ as both human and divine, the Council declared that the person of Jesus was to be understood as 'complete in deity and complete in humanity' and that his two natures were related 'without separation or division' and yet also 'without confusion or change'. My treatment of the relationship between the psychological and the theological seeks to reflect this Chalcedonian pattern.

Faith within a living relationship

Within the literature of psychology, and among the many models underpinning the practices of psychotherapy, there is much theorising about how individuals acquire beliefs about themselves, others and the world. Likewise, psychological processes can easily be invoked to explain the acquisition of religious beliefs. Whatever the approach, all would agree that beliefs are learned. One can no more arrive at a belief system independently than one can expect to be able to speak English if one has been reared by wolves. Certainly we learn our beliefs, our faith, as part of a community of believers. Importantly, it is suggested, we have been inducted into this community, the church, most power- fully within the context of particular relationships: I initially believed, essentially, because a particular other person believed. While this can be explained in psychological terms, as a Christian I claim that my faith, while inseparable from psychological processes, does not arise from provisional human understanding but, rather, is engendered and maintained by the power of the Holy Spirit.

Within relationships we are empowered by the Spirit to assert and proclaim our trust in Christ crucified and risen, in the face of all other understandings, powers and dominions, which might threaten to negate this faith. And this is a living dynamic hope, not a static fixed state. It is transmitted, understood and actualised within, and by the transforming of, the process of relating to others. This hope in action is love. Psychological discourses, however powerful, offer no ulti- mate purpose which defies the threat of suffering, death and oblivion, for they render justice, beauty, love, as ultimately futile values. 'For the creation was subjected to futility, not of its own will but by the will of him who subjected it in hope.' (Rom 8:20).

Regardless of how we first glimpse the Christian hope, the self- authenticating love which promises to transfigure living in relation- ship, this seed will not flourish unless it is nurtured, caught up within the process of a developing relationship with an experienced mentor.

The historical skete as metaphor

Historically, Christian monasticism found one of its earliest ex- pressions in the lives of those who abandoned society to seek and serve God in the harsh isolation of the deserts of fourth century Egypt. Many different experiments to live a celibate life, shed of all distrac- tions to focus on what was most needful, were tried: the solitary life of a hermit, communities of brothers or sisters, and everything in between. But perhaps most notable among these various shapes of living was the tradition of several hermits or monks grouped together as disciples of their spiritual father or *abba* in the *lavra* or *skete*. The collected wisdom of some of these great abbas has been preserved for us in the writings known as the *Sayings of the Desert Fathers*. Much of this wisdom is expressed in stories of the encounters and exchanges between abbas and their pupils, and between abbas. In an introduction to her translation of the *Sayings,* Benedicta Ward attempts to draw out the essence of the spirituality of the desert as a life 'not taught but caught'.

The prayer of these monks was a whole way of life 'continually turned toward God'; and, within the *skete,* 'the role of the 'abba', the spiritual father, was, *vital,* literally, that is to say, 'life-giving'.' The abba, 'was the one who discerned reality and whose words, therefore, gave life ... it was a word that was part of a relationship, a word which would give life to the disciple if it were received.'

Ward goes on to say, 'The Coptic monks were simple men, and their understanding of this relationship is difficult to recapture in sophisticated society.'[2] To suggest a full understanding of these particular relationships from a twenty-first-century vantage would be presumptuous. Nevertheless the image of the *skete* is a potent metaphor capturing a neglected but vital aspect in the development of religious identity. For employing the *skete* thus not only affords continuity with the theme of the process and quality of relationship as central to our religious purpose but also simultaneously invokes the proper and necessary historical, psychological and theological perspectives.[3]

The psychological skete: *dialogue and self-reflection*

The *skete* as a particular didactic relationship works well as a paradigm for the nurturing of psychological maturity. We bring to each meeting with another person our habitual ways of relating. The

2. Benedicta Ward, (translator), *The Sayings of the Desert Fathers,* Mowbray, London, 1975.
3. I owe a particular debt of gratitude to Dr Petà Dunstan, a Church historian and an authority on the development of the Anglican Religious Life. Through our conversations I have absorbed her four-fold schema characterising the full range of activity within the Religious Life. This essay is thus, at least structurally, a contemporary, psychological treatment of Dr Dunstan's historical survey.

outcome may be straightforward and satisfying. Or it may run into problems and we find ourselves frustrated, ignored, put-down, resentful, hurt, angry, dissatisfied. Our first tendency is to attribute blame, most often to the other: 'He's mean, bossy, controlling, domineering, arrogant, self-centred, narcissistic, manipulative; and I'm the decent, caring victim.'

We label ourselves and others in ways which maintain a good self-image, a valued self-identity and our self-esteem. And we carry these expectations of ourselves and the other forward into our next meeting. We become trapped in the reciprocal-roles we engender, and they become self-fulfilling prophecies. Importantly, however, an astute mentor will *not* collude with our efforts to recruit him or her into the complementary role – a role which merely supports our own view of ourselves – rather, in love, we will be challenged.

In psychological terms the task of the psychological abba, or mentor, is essentially to induct his pupil into a new way of relating, a new reciprocal role of mutual respect, collaboration and honesty. His 'tools' are receptivity, empathy and an understanding and acceptance of the other in all the subtle, complex depth of his fallen human nature. For he too has had to learn the courage to face many unwelcome insights, disappointments, humiliations and sufferings on the long and slow path to deep self-knowledge. Significantly, the mentor is not a judge exposing the shortcomings in his pupil – the projections, the real motivations, the power-games or the falsity – for criticism and rebuke. Instead, the uncovering of the workings of our sinful nature in this context of acceptance leads to the beginnings of a freedom from the blind repetition of our habitual ways of relating, an exit from the restrictions of identities which limit us. Crucially, what the mentor is teaching is the capacity for true dialogue with another; and, the skill of dialogue when internalised becomes the capacity for honest self-reflection.

The theological skete: dialogue in the Spirit

The attempt at *genuine* dialogue, is the meeting between persons (not positions), where each, secure enough to recognise the shortcomings in their own partial knowledge, in turn listens deeply and openly, with respect and humility to understand and value what the other is trying to say. In dialogue there is no attempt to win an argument and overpower the other. Rather, in a process of exploring disagreement, an acceptance of the difference and individuality of the other leads to an ever deeper mutual understanding and openness to learn from the other.

Dialogue is indeed a rare skill which needs to be learnt within a particular relationship; moreover, this relationship must be one that eschews all temptation to exert power and influence over the other. To the extent that this can ever be achieved the relationship must instead be underpinned by love, in the power of the Spirit. As such, it is not only a skill but a grace which simultaneously needs to be learned and prayed for in the Spirit.

Intimacy in the Spirit

At the Last Supper, shortly after Jesus had washed his disciples' feet, he said 'I give you a new commandment: love one another; as I have loved you, so you are to love one another. If there is love among you, then all will know that you are my disciples' *(John 13. 34, 35)*. We will be called also into other particular relationships in the religious life where there will be a clearer equality in terms of experience. Traditionally 'particular relationships' have been questioned, if not frowned upon or indeed prohibited, within the religious life. However, as has been discussed above, some degree of intimacy between religious seems essential, and healthy within the context of a psychological maturity, for community life to flourish.

Theological 'love in the Spirit' and psychological intimacy must not be confused, but neither can they be separated. The religious life is a means to an end; and that end is reached through our desire for a living relationship with Christ. Yet, is not our desire for God hidden in our lesser desires, in our living relationships with each other, of our craving for both physical and emotional love and intimacy? 'Intimacy' is a very loaded word, but the question of our true relationship with God *and* with others is not trivial, and ' intimacy' serves well to carry both the promise and danger of our desire to love one another.

The Latin root of intimacy *intimus* means inmost. In intimacy, a sharing of what is inmost, we expose ourselves in a process of reciprocal self-disclosure, mutual concern and care, and a participation in creating new meanings and bonds together. There are various aspects to intimacy – emotional, intellectual, physical – but all need not be pursued within a particular relationship for intimacy to develop. As social animals we need to find a secure human base within a social world, and intimacies are the bonds which create this psychological security. But the impulse, the desire for intimacy does not guarantee the making, maintaining and deepening of our affectional bonds. The psychological forces are powerful and must be engaged with carefully and with respect if they are not to become distorted or even destructive of the fabric of our community life.

In all this, we cannot prescribe the action of the Holy Spirit. Rather, we can only be receptive to the will of God. Yet if the *skete* is our heritage, then we might hope that when we both have been stripped of our fantasies and projections, when we know the subtleties of our drives for power and our self-deception, when we meet as equals recognising our brokenness, insufficiency and need, then there can be, by the grace of God, and despite ourselves, a true encounter of 'inmost with inmost'. Would not this be a sacred meeting with each *other* in which the *Other* was disclosed? Would not this true meeting between persons be not only a point of transmission of our faith, but also a place between and among us where hope and love, through Christ, in the power of the Holy Spirit, was continually manifested, renewed and deepened? And what would religious identity mean then in a relationship stretched beyond our known, safe identities? To answer these questions, we must now turn to an account of our individual relationship with Christ in prayer.

PRAYER AND EVERYTHING ELSE

Dialogue, obedience and process
Our effort to pray, understood as 'a life continually turned toward

God' (Ward, 1975), is the prime activity of the religious. We hear the call of God, the promise of a love that will satiate our desire, and turn to that voice in obedience to his will. Yet, when we responded to the call initially, none of us had a full understanding of our destination. The first inklings are associated with the beginnings of an honest self-knowledge learned in relationship through the process of dialogue. Genuine dialogue within a relationship is a listening and learning and a preparedness to respond and be changed. This is our obedience. It is this same process of dialogue, or obedience, which will characterise our initiation into genuine prayer: the unfolding of our relationship with Christ in the power of the Spirit who will lead us into all truth. This suggests a linear progression from the dialogue of the *skete* to the dialogue of prayer. More correctly, the two processes inevitably move contiguously, always cross-fertilising each other in an ongoing dialectic relationship – our relationship with each other, and our relationship in prayer with Christ must not be confused, but neither can they be separated.

Dialogue and the work of prayer

Although the quintessential expression of prayer may be thought to be individual and contemplative, much of our time is absorbed in our corporate prayer of the Eucharist and the Divine Office: saying the psalms, the reading of scripture and hymn-singing. We also study the Bible, read works of spirituality and theology and reflect upon the lives of the saints. Again it is productive to regard these activities as involving a process of dialogue: listening, reflecting and responding in a mutual exchange with the person of Christ in the power of the Spirit. For the danger is of standing *over* Scripture (and other texts) and deciding what they mean solely from within the perspective of our human spirit and as the 'world' knows things to be. Instead, we are called to stand *under* Scripture in an engagement (in the Spirit) which will continually reshape, transform and renew our hearts and minds (see e.g. Romans 12.2).

Too often we become lazy in what we believe. We stop questioning through fear of doubt or because of our determination to hold a party line. But the Eucharist, the Divine Office, and scripture should be vital 'words' for us. If they are not then questions need to be asked. But we must do so in the expectation that the answer will be inspired by the Spirit. Such a dialogue will not necessarily be comfortable or happy. It may lead us into doubt and confusion; but also into addressing – over and over again – questions of real importance: the meaning of our life, of love, of power, of suffering, of death. And the Spirit will lead us through our questioning to radically new, life-giving answers that we do not yet know or understand. Moreover, our understanding of the Gospel, faith, worship, mission, the Church must also continually flow anew from our living engagement in dialogue with Scripture, and in all our prayer.

Individual prayer: a process of relationship

In our individual prayer, while we may properly acknowledge God as mysterious, beyond us, transcendent, we have no other approach for communication than that between persons. We are obliged to make this imaginative leap to 'speak' to God in prayer. Given our description of interpersonal relating in terms of reciprocal-roles, we inevitably may bring some of these same dynamics into our efforts to engage in a relationship with God. This may be especially true if these hidden reciprocal-roles come charged with strong emotion. Our 'prayer' may be engaging in an emotive internal dialogue between elements of ourselves, notwithstanding the feeling that we are indeed communicating with a spiritual presence.

Christianity is awash with theological images which, if pursued in isolation from one another, all too readily lend themselves to be confused with the dissociated psychological elements in us. For example, our fear of the judgement of an all-powerful God, King and Father and our feelings of guilt, may be derived from the powerful psychological feelings we experienced as children in relation to inappropriately critical or demanding parents. Our prayer may then simply become an exercise in still trying to placate Mum and Dad: being good in the way they expected us to be good. And the fruit of our prayer will be merely a perpetuation of the values of, for example, middle class culture, rather than their radical transformation through the Good News of the Glory of Christ crucified and raised from the dead.

A yet more subtle distortion of the Gospel is a psychological idealisation of the Love of God: a fantasised set of reciprocal-roles in which I am perfectly loved and cared for by a perfect loving and caring parent. Theologically, the Divine Love, Agape, from the Father, through the Son, in the Power of the Holy Spirit is perfect. But we must not confuse that with the experience of human love where perfect love is a fantasy – the fantasy that, when disillusioned, complains 'How can a truly loving God let little children suffer?' Our faith actually begins by raising suffering and death upon a cross before us, to reveal the profound mystery of God's love: the love which empowers us to hope still in the face of everything that threatens to negate hope and life and light. This Love does not excuse us from suffering; indeed, it was only revealed at its deepest and fullest in the place of suffering.

The dialogue of the *skete*, a process in which we come to know that we are listened to in love and we learn to listen, prepares us for prayer. In the *skete* we are slowly stripped of our role-playing and we come to a more essential recognition of the other. This recognition in love is not a narrowing of our appreciation of the other, a condensing of his or her essence but rather a disclosure, an opening up of the essential wide and deep mystery of the other, the mystery of the very otherness of the other. Our listening to God in prayer similarly is a stripping of preconceptions about ourselves and about God which leads not to our capture of some objective knowledge of God, or to the quick fulfilment of our distorted human desires, or into power, but to the gradual transfiguration of our humanity in the face of the mystery of God – a gaze which invites us ever more deeply into communion through Christ in the power of the Holy Spirit.

Yet how exactly does God speak to us in prayer? How does he manage to slip past our distorted expectations and inform us? Psychologically, the simplistic model of reciprocal-roles, which suggests that the individuality of the self is a fiction plastering over multiple identities lodged in multiple relationships is, ultimately, untenable. For my brain can function creatively to achieve integration, new self-knowledge over and above the internal dialogue of experientially learned reciprocal-roles. Theologically, however, we attribute this imaginative creativity of hearing God 'speak' to the action of the Spirit. And our theological 'test' would be that the relationship of love (not power) that we are led into is such that a deepening love of God is never at the expense of, but is revealed in, our deepening love of others. It is an insight and a love which cannot separate Divine Love and human love yet does not confuse them.

Identity in prayer

However intimate becomes our relationship in the *skete*, we are only human and to some extent we will hold back some of the truth about ourselves. But we are completely transparent to the one who created us and who has watched over our every step in life. Moreover, God sees first and foremost not a monk or nun, a friar or sister, but the unique individual upon whom he has set his heart and for whom he has gone before to prepare a path into new life. Each inner journey, arising from different temperamental make-ups, the different past experiences of life and relationships of each, and perhaps God's different plans for each, will thus be different. Life in the Spirit nurtures individuality. For dialogue is always about holding the tension between togetherness, oneness and separateness, complete otherness; between equality with Jesus, the incarnate Christ on the cross, and humility before the majesty of the Creator of time and space and all things who meets us there. Nevertheless, mindful of the witness of those who have gone before us in the Christian way, we will expect that, in our common relationship with Christ, we will come to the same freeing insights and share in the same new pattern of life.

The intimate dialogue of prayer begun and nurtured in the *skete* will draw us more deeply into the knowledge of God's acceptance of us as we are: confused and sinful; and God's loving judgement of us: not a condemnation but a freedom to acknowledge the truth about ourselves. By the grace of God we will be strengthened to repent, and

He will forgive us again and again and again: we will learn God's faithfulness in this commitment to our relationship with him despite our betrayal, denial and rejection of him. God desires us but will not coerce or overwhelm or subsume us into the 'awfulness' of his Being.

On the cross, God assumes our broken powerlessness and meets us there, so that the mustard seed of Love might be exposed as the most precious gift. And we are changed. This new Love eclipsing our psychological need for the care and security of a parent and our will to power, and transfiguring the psychologically ideal lover into a radically new living relationship in the Spirit is new life. This is our true identity: the mystery of our relationship with the One on the Cross. We are made in the image of God, and that image is the Glory of Christ crucified and risen.

RETURNING TO THE WORLD

From the skete *to community*

There is a real danger that when we put on the habit we become what we are supposed to be in the mind of the world, and so fail to find our true identity in the mind of Christ (1 Cor 2:14-16). This new life-giving relationship grows most especially in the *skete*: particular relationships, rooted and nurtured within the context of our solitary prayer. Here we are changed. We are changed too as we branch out taking the gift of love, crucified and risen, into the dialogue of our many other relationships within community. Moreover, the corporate body of the community is then transformed to become a place of dialogue and generosity: of *obedience;* a place of honesty, maturity, intimacy, forgiveness and faithfulness in relationship: of *chastity;* a place of freedom from the pursuit and appropriation of the things of the world: of *poverty.* This also is a slow, lifelong process because corporately, as well as individually, the renunciation and sacrifice of the religious life involves first knowing our old false identities through and through and 'owning' them. For we cannot sacrifice what we do not own ourselves completely. Yet, though we may then see our failings, we have no power of our own to change the quality of our corporate life. It is only in the Spirit that we are enabled to offer up the old for sacrifice. From within the perspective of the secular world, the sacrifice of the religious life is seen as a neurotic if not bizarre subjugation of the human spirit. But in the Spirit we see that in our relationship with Christ we sacrifice, and are sacrificed, for Love. This is the vocation of all Christians, and the sign of our corporate meeting with Love is the '*skete*' of the Eucharist.

Religious and faith in the world

Finally, our relationship with those outside the community is changed. The mustard tree extends its branches wide into society renewing our multiple relationships there, and further enriching the religious identity. We bring to our relationships with the institution of the Church, with Christians of other denominations, and with peoples of other faiths this same essential capacity for dialogue in the Spirit, witnessing to our experience of the life-giving power of the Cross.

And we must also go out to meet the secular world. A true loving relationship is borne of mutual self-giving and receiving, but learning to love and serve the other also requires the growth both of a knowledge of the other and of self-knowledge – again, dialogue.

Whether active or contemplative, we are all unavoidably enmeshed in the contemporary world. It is a romantic illusion to believe that we can creditably absent ourselves from engagement with money, power and privilege; the issues of social justice, discrimination, the economic exploitation of others and of the physical destruction of our environment; or from our social and political responsibilities. If we are to learn how best to offer our service in the world then, in our prayer and action, we must be informed not only about the other, but also recognise our own culpability. Then we can return to the world in honesty and hand back to our culture its constricting projections. Sharing a common psychological humanity, we can 'come out' as ordinary, flawed individuals who nevertheless are empowered to live and proclaim the Good News of the mystery of Christ crucified and risen, the transforming source of all justice, truth, love, joy and peace.

A postscript

Religious will be familiar already with three of the four principal elements in this discussion: the solitary relationship with God in prayer, community life and the relationship with, and work of service to, the world. The life of the *skete* may be recognised as those special relationships in our life which have significantly influenced and formed us, even when the meetings have been informal, brief or simply so ordinary that their fundamental importance at the time was missed. It has been argued that the intimacy of the *skete* should be consciously brought forward as an essential element of our lives, of equal importance alongside private prayer and study, corporate living and worship, and work in the world.

In addition, the suggestion would be made that, for the healthy development of any community, indeed any individual religious vocation, a conscious pursuit of all four aspects of the religious life should be undertaken, in one form or another. This, after all, is surely the multiple vocation and common pathway for all Christians.

This essay has attempted to plot a rough course of the development of religious identity from the first stages of a contemporary religious vocation. The tidy progression from 'habit' through 'community' to ' *skete*' and 'prayer', and back to community and out to the world, does not reflect the reality of the interdependent development and integration of these different aspects of identity. There are different relationships, yet all are being led by the Spirit on a journey into the depth of the cross and resurrection life: the heart of the living God wherein we find our true identity.

NINE

Praying in a Monastery

NICOLAS CR

'Why did you decide to become a monk?' is a question young people often ask when they visit us. 'Because I wanted to pray' is the answer they usually get. It sounds a pat response and perhaps an entirely expected one – praying is what people expect monks and nuns to do. They also think we are particularly good at it. Pictures of monks apparently wrapped in prayer gazing at a crucifix; or images of habited figures in a darkened choir chanting the office suggest that prayer comes naturally and easily to us, and takes up a large part of the day. It is sometimes quite a surprise to people when they learn that religious men and women must do quite a lot of things other than pray, and are often hard-pressed to find the time – even more the energy – to do it properly. Very few of the men and women who have taken on the monastic life will admit to having no problems in prayer or would agree that the appearance of calm, ordered, utterly attentive devotion which the stock pictures suggest, bears much relationship to what is going on in our minds at the times we do pray. This is complicated by the fact that the promise of what prayer is going to be like hardly ever bears much relationship to the reality as we experience it once we are in community.

My own first visits to the community I later joined were times of intense and satisfying prayer. I wandered round in a daze. Everything seemed to speak of God. Each crucifix was almost alive. The chapel had a warm, inviting prayerfulness about it that made me content to spend hours there. At Mass I could almost see the angels standing round the altar. If this was the foretaste of prayer, I thought, the living of it would be heaven.

Within a few years that experience had faded. By then I was a priest, immensely happy on a mission station with several churches, hundreds of devoted Christians to care for, in lovely country and with the excitement of doing this all in the midst of a civil war. The question of religious life was still there – but pushed a little to one side while I got on with this mission life. But the civil war quickly ceased to be a game. People got killed; people I knew were murdered. Various attempts were made to negotiate peace, but none worked. As the war heated up, the lies increased, the madness multiplied; and the people who suffered most were the village people who had no defence against the armed men of either side. Only prayer, I thought, could bring an end to this madness. When violence forced me to leave my mission station I knew that my time had come.

That little bit of autobiography provides some important questions. For whose benefit do we pray? Is it for ourselves, or for others? If prayer is, as my early experience suggested, deeply fulfilling of the love which exists between us and God, should we not always enjoy it? Yet if prayer is to be for others I must pursue it as work done for others, whether I like it or not. And beyond that is the question: Why enter a religious community in order to pray? Can't all Christians pray? That is an important question since it is not only the large amount of time given to prayer that makes monastic prayer what it is. It is the nature of the monastic life which tries to dissolve the boundaries between activity and prayer so that the whole life participates in the prayer which Christ is offering constantly for the whole world.

All religious communities pray, just as all Christians pray. And all will give it a priority in their life. Yet they will see it differently and give differing amounts of time, or differing orders of priority to their prayer. Sometimes the community is best known for its works, and the works can be extremely busy and demanding. The problem then becomes one of how to fit in the prayer. Indeed, how does prayer 'fit in'? It is not enough that sisters or brethren simply say the office. Nor is it enough simply to say it together. All religious recognise the need for it to be said well, attentively, with concern that it should be a fitting offering of praise to the God who created us, redeemed us and called us to this life. Corporate prayer in a community is where the life of the community is centred. No one can understand what the life is about without having some grasp of the nature of corporate prayer.

In the first place, it offers to God that praise which he is due and which it is our greatest joy to give. We love God, and if we don't feel we love him very much we try to love him more. Every person who loves another person likes to think of that other person, to remember her looks, to think of his kindness, to laugh gently at her humour, to think of ways of pleasing him. That is the first motive for our prayer. God has created us. Everything we have – the world around us, the family and friends, the food, the breath of life in us – comes to us as a gift from God. We did not deserve it. We could never earn it. God simply gave it to us, and even though we still live lives that are so far from deserving the kindness and gifts of God, he goes on giving them to us, because he loves us. Nothing can ever describe the extent of the love of God. We can only be amazed and wonder, and adore a God who loves as he loves.

Yet we must be realistic. Few of us feel this about God all the time. Prayer gets jaded, becomes a chore, an empty time spent, or a time not spent. Each of us needs to keep reminding ourselves that in some sense prayer should be a joy since it is entering into the love of One who loves us. When we discover it has ceased to be a joy we may need to refresh it, to turn back to scripture, to go into retreat, to change the nature of our reading. Or we may need to understand it differently and discover that the joy is still there but is now to be found on a deeper level. The more easily recognised pleasure in prayer which happens on the surface is replaced by a deep conviction of rightness, of purpose. Love centres on the will and our love may need to go through quite a long purging process until it becomes a love which is truly for God alone and not for the pleasure we may extract from his love. 'I am the true vine and my Father is the vine-dresser ... every branch of mine that does bear fruit he prunes that it may bear more fruit.'[1] There is no promise we shall enjoy the pruning; but as the pruning takes place, we realise there is a greater freedom, a purer air, a larger horizon and we

1. Jn 15:1,2

sense a deepening of our love for God.

Yet we don't love God on our own. Other people also love God and we find ourselves joined with them by our love. That gives a particular kind of joy to praying together. We are talking together about the person we all love, not in competition but in delight that this beloved person is one we can all share. Day after day we sing the psalms which for over two thousand years have been one of the chief means of praising God. 'Bless the Lord, O my soul, and all that is within me bless his holy name!'[2] Yet we do not only praise but pray that our perception of his goodness will increase. 'Open my eyes that I may see, the wonders of your law.'[3] Even complaint, at which the Jews were very good, enters into this prayer. 'Thou hast made us the taunt of our neighbours, the derision and scorn of those round about us ... All this has come upon us, though we have not forgotten thee, or been false to thy covenant.'[4] And then there is sorrow as we realise that after all, we really have been false to our promise. 'Have mercy on me, O God, according to thy steadfast love.'[5]

At the same time, the Scripture readings and the feasts of the Church bring before us the events in which God has shown his love and determination that we will be saved. Each day the Song of Zechariah and the Song of Mary are sung, or said to remind us of God's gift of Christ in the child Jesus. How little deserving we ever were of any gift; yet God gave us his most precious gift, his own Son, Himself and we hear his teaching read to us; we hear of the miracles he performed out of compassion; we receive the revelation he gave us of the nature of his Father in heaven, and then to our shame we hear how we crucified him. For not just once, two thousand years ago was Jesus crucified. He is crucified daily, by us in our sins. We can never, like the pharisee in the gospel story,[6] thank God that we are not as other people are. We too have sinned and must always repent. Yet forgive-

2. Ps 103:1
3. Ps 119:18
4. Ps 44:13.17
5. Ps 51:1
6. Lk 18:9 ff

ness is offered and we know ourselves to be still the cherished sons and daughters of God, destined for life eternal, with him in a glory which we can barely begin to glimpse now.

All this is celebrated in every Office that we pray. We give thanks. We are reminded of what God has done. We learn together who we are. We look round and see that we are part of a company, members of the body of Christ; and as members of that body we find Christ is praying with us, in us. Our prayer becomes his prayer; our weak feelings, stumbling words, uncertain thoughts are taken up in his and prayer becomes a sharing in the love which Christ himself has for the Father.

This brings us to the second gift which corporate prayer has to give us. It becomes the means by which God works in us that miracle of salvation which makes us what he wants us to be. We are not alone in the Christian life. Jesus made it clear that we always have brothers and sisters for whom we must care and for whom we give our lives. Jesus himself said, 'Greater love has no man than this, that a man lay down his life for his friends.'[7] Few of us are called to an obvious martyrdom but a religious life which is not lived far more for others than for oneself quickly becomes self-centred, self-indulgent and corrupt. An awareness that, in entering this life, we are laying down our own lives for others helps greatly to keep the focus where it should be. Often then, when the life becomes difficult, because of sickness, because of problems in community, because of the nature of the work, we see that it is the sheer difficulty itself in which the laying down of our life for others becomes fruitful. We are not alone in this. We are a pilgrim people and if many of the pilgrims look to us, individually, for help we also look to each other for the support and guidance we need along our road. It comes in strange ways.

It is well known in any community that when relationships break down, the break-down will show itself in the recitation of the psalms. Psalms can only be sung together if we listen carefully to each other. None of us can take the lead. None of us can assert himself or herself.

7. Jn 15:13

We have to listen, to let other people lead us and to care enough about them to ensure that they are with us as we pray. That is a discipline, a constant check on the selfishness which is inherent in our make-up. If we find ourselves out of step with the psalmody, we are probably out of step too with our lives. If we are attending, we will then find ourselves saying the Lord's Prayer and wondering if we really can expect to be forgiven our sins, when we are still holding the grievance of other people's sins in our hearts.

There is a third aspect of corporate prayer of which we can only speak with diffidence. It is the way it affects other people who visit us. Our worship is never our own. It is offered to God and it is God who often does things with it which amaze us. This may be expressed in a kind of parable. Our Community Church has a vaulted ceiling which provides a marvellous singing acoustic. The sound we make in choir is taken up, rolled along this roof, magnified and sometimes, it seems, purified and comes down on the visitors as a lovely offering of traditional monastic prayer. Yet we hear little of it ourselves! We cannot bask in any supposed glory of the wonderful sound we are making since we do not hear it; but our visitors often find in it an experience of God such as they have never known before. They will be refreshed and sometimes inspired and when we hear of it we can only be convinced that, somewhere, God has been involved using our very flawed offering to show himself again to someone who needed him.

When we speak in this way of prayer we speak of an ideal. The ideal is always there and exists, and the knowledge that it is true is what makes it possible for us sometimes to feel it in its fulness, more often to catch glimpses of it along the way. Most of the time, of course, we are struggling. We fumble with the music, give up in disgust when the singing goes too high; find our thoughts have been far away for almost the whole Office or just sit in sullen rebellion because we are angry or hurt. Curiously enough, this is not a failure to make the Office what it is. Prayer in community is not only real when it achieves the kind of perfection which an orchestra or Bach choir may aim at. In fact, it will not be real if it is only performance.

Prayer needs to be real, but what makes it real? Those of us who live in community know that the realness of prayer comes from the community. As I write this, I watch a brother outside the window making a compost heap. All kinds of rubbish are being gathered up in the grounds and dumped on it. As the weeks go by, the heap gets bigger and blacker. It gets turned over, steams gently and gives off a smell. Out of this compost will come the roses and the vegetables that fill our garden during the summer. In much the same way prayer draws all of our life into itself and extends into every part of it. Tensions, rows, tiredness, joys, laughter and everything that makes up human life become the stuff of prayer. That is the sense in which religious communities are praying communities – not because they give a lot of time to prayer, but because by the nature of the vows every part of their life becomes a part of the offering to God. Visitors, political problems, society all get drawn into the life; so the prayer which takes place in choir is firmly rooted in this soil and at the same time offers it to God.

Prayer in choir needs to be seen as a living river. Into it come all kinds of tributaries. All the brothers or sisters bring their own contributions, their own concerns, their joys and anxieties. Visitors add another dimension. The music, especially if it is one of the ancient forms of chant, roots the worship in the Christian tradition stretching back to the earliest centuries of the Christian world. The words of Scripture go back beyond that into Israel's long and anguished experience of living with their God.

Yet the worship is not backward looking, except to remind us of the graciousness of God. The river moves onwards, taking us into the future. For us, the future has two dimensions. One is the future of life in this world. The other is the eschatological future where we will be taken into the divine life of the Godhead and know the unspeakable joys of the vision of God. In regard to the first future, our prayer embraces the troubles of the nations which we see torn apart by greed and violence, and seeks to find a way forward for them into greater life and stability. It sees the ecological disaster threatening the world and prays that God will show us a way round that. It picks up the lives of individual men and women who are in distress, of people who suffer from the social problems of our age, the drugs, the AIDS virus, unemployment and despair. It shares, too, in the excitement of new discoveries in the world of science.

Increasingly today our worship is informed by art and drama, by new and imaginative ways of expressing our desires in liturgy. The bleak, bald liturgies of the early liturgical reforms have been replaced by prayers in which beautiful English has joined ancient concepts and modern insights. The suspicion of anything that was not immediately and obviously 'meaningful' has given way to an appreciation of symbolism, and the need for worship to engage on intuitive and sensory levels as well as the cerebral. Our place of worship becomes a workshop in which ideas are tested out, new expressions of old doctrines are crafted in modern words. Church, choir and monastic services unite timelessness to a vigorous engagement with the present. Prayer moves beyond the repetition of words and becomes life.

Just as life itself is complex and many-sided so too is prayer. As a person grows in prayer, more of it will be identified with life in a way which makes it often difficult to distinguish one from the other. Often, Christians find themselves joined through the body of Christ with the needs and prayers of others. We pray for those in despair; we must not be surprised if we ourselves often experience despair. We suffer in illness; we are not far wrong if we use our pain as a means of praying for others who suffer in illness. We find ourselves surrounded by a hostile world; when we still see hope in God and joy in a God-created world, we may be bringing that hope and joy into the world for others. And when we ourselves in religious communities find ourselves under great pressure we must not be surprised to realise it is the prayers of others inside, or often outside the community that hold us onto God. We cannot be too proud to admit our need for other people's prayer.

This is the work of intercession which every community must see as a work that needs constantly to be done. It is a work, and it can often feel like a work as one goes through names, thinks about people's suffering and argues with God over some of the larger problems of the world which we are called to pray for.

Yet the work is also a privilege. Here in some mysterious way we are invited to work with God. None of us ever knows how our prayers are used. None of us understands the mechanics of how prayer 'works'. We can only tell God in humility about the cares we want him to do something about and trust the rest to him. Yet that itself expresses a relationship with God, that of the father and child. We trust him. We come to him with our needs. Many will tell us it is a waste of time; why should God be bothered with such small things? If he is good he will do good things and he will not be influenced by our little desires. There is a logic in that, but the heart tells us otherwise. Jesus himself told us otherwise. 'Ask and it will be given to you'.[8] Jesus showed us a God who is a Father who loves to receive requests from his children since that shows that they love him. Out of his love he responds, and extraordinary things can happen.

Yet if we are to pray as children of God our prayers will make no sense unless our lives in Community reflect the truth that we are alive in one body and that Body is Christ. One of the hardest parts of community life is simply to live the Gospel. 'Be ye perfect,' said Jesus, 'as your heavenly father is perfect'.[9] It is hard to understand this. Anyone who strives after a perfect keeping of the rules will find either a self-righteous conceit over an imagined perfection achieved, or will despair at completing a task which never can be done. Yet the aim really is to be like the Father whom Jesus reveals to us. In a sense one could say that the whole aim of monastic life, as of Christian life is to take seriously Paul's great desire 'that Christ be formed in you.'[10] To love as he loves, to forgive as he forgives, is to be perfect. Such love and such forgiveness will be completely unself-regarding. It will be infinitely fruitful within the community for it will be the presence of Christ who alone truly loves and forgives as the Father loves and

8. Mt 7:7
9. Mt 5:48
10. Gal 4:19

forgives. It will also make the community a place where the anger and hatred, the unforgiving nature of human life can be absorbed and peace can be found. Elsewhere Jesus says, 'If you are offering your gift at the altar and there remember that your brother has something against you ... go; first be reconciled to your brother ... '[11] Community life needs to be lived constantly against this standard if its prayer is to be the life-enhancing, peace-giving prayer of Jesus.

In the end, that is the prayer we must want. When we reach that place, then every word from God becomes a delight. 'Oh, how I love thy law; all the day long is my study in it,' cries the psalmist.[12] 'How sweet are thy words to my taste; sweeter than honey to my mouth.'[13] Religious life is full of all kinds of activity – work to keep going, pastoral concerns, preaching, study, recreation, holidays, house chores and missionary work. Yet none of us should forget that our real reason for being in this life is to seek God, and in seeking him to find him. In finding him we explore his ways, we follow a road that he has chosen for us, we learn how he loves us. It is the desire for God that keeps us praying and the hope that in the end nothing else will matter, no sacrifice will turn out to have been too great; no pain endured and no joy passed by will be remembered in the wonder of seeing him face to face and knowing his love as it really is.

11. Mt 5:23
12. Ps 119:97
13. Ps 119:103

TEN

Love Bade Me Welcome

EMMA ssc

Love bade me welcome: yet my soul drew back,
　　Guilty of dust and sin.
But quick-eyed Love, observing me grow slack
　　From my first entrance in,
Drew nearer to me, sweetly questioning,
　　If I lacked any thing.

A guest, I answered, worthy to be here:
　　Love said, You shall be he.
I the unkind, ungrateful? Ah my dear,
　　I cannot look on thee.
Love took my hand, and smiling did reply,
　　Who made the eyes but I?

Truth Lord, but I have marred them: let my shame
　　Go where it doth deserve.
And know you not, says Love, who bore the blame?
　　My dear, then I will serve.
You must sit down, says Love, and taste my meat:
　　So I did sit and eat.

George Herbert [1]

LOVE BIDS US WELCOME

George Herbert's poem expresses poignantly the encounter of the human soul with the love of God. Through dialogue with our human nature, Love enables us to respond to the invitation to taste its 'meat'.

1. 'Love bade me welcome', in *The Works of George Herbert*, (1st pub.) Oxford University Press, Oxford, 1941, p. 188.

Our witness as Christians to this relationship with the source of love takes various forms in the religious life. In this essay, I would like to share some thoughts on this journey as a recently professed member of a contemplative community, where the focus is our shared life of prayer and worship. I have found this life creates a place of welcome where others can experience and share in God's hospitality. The psalmist wrote, 'My merciful God comes to meet me'.[2] In the person of Jesus Christ, humanity has encountered the fullness of the welcome of God's love. Those who, as recorded in the Gospels, responded to this welcome were the ones Jesus was able to welcome into the Kingdom of God. They were not those who were approved of by the religious authorities, and it is significant that it was their welcoming of Jesus that caused a transformation in their lives. It wasn't that they had to change their lives in order to welcome him. Zacchaeus welcomed Jesus into his home and then declared what changes he was going to make in his life.[3] Jesus' response was, 'Today salvation has come to this house.' The woman who anointed Jesus' feet [4] was able to 'love much' because she was open to Jesus' total welcome of her. Jesus contrasted the welcome he received from her with that of his host, who had in reality not welcomed him, closed as he was within his preconceived ideas about others. Jesus' warning to the religious of his day was, 'The tax-collectors and prostitutes are entering the kingdom of heaven ahead of you.' [5]

The greatest, most significant, example of one who welcomed God must be Mary the Mother of Jesus, referred to, in the Orthodox Church, as God-bearer, *Theotokos*; and I will be referring to her often in this essay.

The parallels between Herbert's poem and Jesus' parable of the Prodigal Son [6] are clear. We have forgotten who we are in our wandering. We have lost touch with the fact that we were created by

2. Ps 59: 10
3. Lk 19: 1-10
4. Lk 7: 36-50
5. Mt 21:31
6. Lk 15:11-32

Love and so belong to Love, who gives our lives their meaning and purpose. Therefore we are taken aback and left speechless by the welcome we receive when we begin to remember and to return. We experience the sense of returning home. Love is the only power which can truly convert us and bring us to our knees.

Love's welcome is experienced as Love's choosing of us. Although impartial and unbounded, Love always chooses. We are valuable and infinitely precious because God has chosen us, each in a unique way, 'before the creation of the world'.[7] A story by Jesuit and spiritual teacher, the late Anthony de Mello, illustrates how, when we experience being accepted and loved as we are right now, we are set free and thus can grow into our fuller potential:

> I was anxious and depressed and selfish. Everyone kept telling me to change … I wanted to change, but simply couldn't, no matter how hard I tried… Then one day [my best friend] said to me, 'Don't change. I love you just as you are.'
>
> I relaxed. I came alive. And suddenly I changed!
>
> Now I know that I couldn't really change until I found someone who would love me whether I changed or not.
>
> Is that how you love me, God?[8]

Like the Prodigal Son, we tend to expect judgement, and critical judgement at that. We are surprised and unmasked by the welcome of Love. A photograph I once saw has stayed with me as an icon of this encounter of Love with our hidden fearful selves. It showed an unarmed protester, walking, arms outstretched, towards a semicircle of armed soldiers, whose guns were all pointing at him. Just to picture it in one's mind's eye can cause a response of recognition deep within oneself. The man was compelled towards his antagonists and he could not help himself. It reminds me that Love draws close to us, unarmed, facing our inner defensive weaponry – revealing our violence in its gentleness.

---

7. Eph 1:4
8. In *The Song of the Bird*, by A. de Mello, S.J., Image Book, 1984, pp. 67-68.

In the light of this all-encompassing Love, we see that human failure is held and in fact becomes creative. We are enabled to see our lives in the light of this love and are given a longing for love's fulfilment in us. 'At the evening of our lives, we will be judged by love,' wrote St John of the Cross. The judgment will be by the love of God which is within our own deepest selves, because love is the very stuff out of which we are made. It is the core of our being. St Mechtilde of Magdeburg wrote, 'You speak to me of my beginnings? I will tell you. I was created in love.' And as Julian discovers in her 'showings': 'love was his meaning … ' So, it is the fullness of this reality that we will become aware of 'when all is revealed'.

BECOMING PART OF LOVE'S WELCOME

'Love bade me welcome' can also be read as Love bidding me *to* welcome. Love sets us free to become a part of Love's welcome of others. As the author of the First Letter of St John wrote to the receiving Church, 'Dear friends, let us love one another, for love comes from God'.[9] Our finding ourselves known by Love opens us onto the deeper reality of which we are all a part: a meeting in the true sense where we are all held in the intimacy of Love, able to see the reality of another, not just through our own needs and perceptions. This is God's doing. We cannot create intimacy with one another, we can only make room for it to happen. Otherwise, it is our moving towards the other with an agenda in place, usually dominated by our felt needs. We have to approach empty-handed in order truly to meet the other.

God welcomes us into the friendship 'feast' of life, as expressed in Herbert's poem. This has obvious echoes with the Eucharist, the celebration of our being drawn together by God in Christ, of the whole creation being gathered up in Christ's offering. This unity we have in Christ was prayed for by Jesus before his death. On the night before he died, Jesus prayed for those who will believe through the teaching of his disciples: 'May they be one, just as you are in me, Father, and

---

9. 1 Jn 4:7

I am in you. May they be in us that the world may believe that you sent me.'[10] Our dwelling in the welcome of God, the very life of the Trinity, itself causes the world to believe, to see the dynamic of God's saving purposes in Jesus. Through it, God's welcome to all is mysteriously proclaimed, shown, enacted. In community, therefore, if we are already united in Christ, it is not a question of our creating community, but becoming sensitive to, discovering, opening in trust to the communion which is already there.

So, God's welcome creates community. We become places of hospitality for others, where they may find the freedom to be themselves. Spiritual writer the late Henri Nouwen has a beautiful passage in his book *The Wounded Healer*:

> When we are not afraid to enter into our own centre and to concentrate on the stirrings of our own soul, we come to know that being alive means being loved. This experience tells us that we can love only because we are born out of love, that we can give only because our life is a gift, and that we can make others free only because we are set free by God whose heart is greater than ours. When we have found the anchor places for our lives in our own centre, we can be free to let others enter into the space created for them and allow them to dance their own dance, sing their own song, and speak their own language without fear. Then our presence is no longer threatening and demanding but inviting and liberating.[11]

Guests and visitors to religious houses frequently talk about the welcome they experience there: the place itself and the life of the community offer a space where they can be themselves. It is important in our present culture, in which so much emphasis is put on communication, to provide people with the opportunity to be quiet, to pray, to make room within for God, to welcome Love's reality in their lives. The paradox is that the more space we give to this welcoming of Love, the more of ourselves is then free to be shared with others and the

---

10. Jn 17:21
11. In *The Wounded Healer*, by Henri Nouwen, Image Books, Doubleday, NY, 1990, p. 91.

deeper and more creative our communication with others will be.

The warmth and generosity of our welcome, in practical and other ways, is an important part of our hospitality to visitors and indeed to one another; but these too can only genuinely spring from our own dwelling in this welcome of Love.

Whenever we pray for another we are making room for them, giving space and time to their reality within our own, and opening a door to God's purposes for us both. St John the Baptist described himself as the friend of the Bridegroom, Christ, who was coming to meet humanity as his Bride. He stepped aside when Jesus appeared, making room for the reality of Christ in the world. So, as well as affecting the way we pray, opening our lives to the reality of another also widens intercession to include the way we live our lives. Our lives are inextricably linked; and the way we live profoundly affects not only those immediately around us, but also others with whom we share our world. Our intercession thus includes our stewardship, the way we think about and use our resources, and our awareness of how this affects others. All that we have, we have received freely as gift from God. Making room for God to work in other people's lives is part of our involvement in the bringing in of God's 'commonwealth' of justice and peace.

CHANNELS OF LOVE'S GRACE

The saints – those whom the Church recognises as communicating something central to us about God and his encounter with humanity – can be seen to have responded to this welcome with everything they had and were, and made room for it in their lives. For example, St Augustine, writing of his conversion, the realisation of God's saving presence in his life, declared to God, 'You were with me but I was not with you'. St Thérèse of Lisieux wrote: 'Merit does not consist in doing or in giving much, but rather in receiving, in loving much.' St Hildegard of Bingen referred to herself as a feather on the breath of God, responding freely to each movement of God within her. St John Chrysostom wrote: '[The one] who is loved wanders in the heart of the lover without any fear.' Father Benson wrote: 'the saints are not those who have done the most for Jesus, but those who have suffered Jesus to do the most for them.'[12] As such, they have become channels of God's welcome to us, revealing his surprising nearness and desire to speak to us. They communicate to us God's grace.

Mary, the Mother of Christ, fulfils a special role, holding within us the space which opens up when we experience God's welcome; embracing within us the Christ-child. She helps us to see that we are held in love. We do not have to hold on; in fact, we are called to let go of our desire to control. The whole world, the whole of creation is held by Love. Within this holding, we can discover our part in the whole, the place which is uniquely ours and yet is also part of the greater picture. Mary holds the Body of Christ in the world in all that that means – the Church, the body of humanity, the body of all that is created – for all has been gathered up by Christ into God. As such, she can help us to find God, resting in her embrace:

> 1 wait in Mary-darkness, faith's walled place
> with hope's expectance of nativity.
>
> I knew for long she carried me and fed me,
> guarded and loved me, though I could not see.
> But only now, with inward jubilee
> I come upon earth's most amazing knowledge:
> *someone is hidden in the dark with me.*[13]

Mary's 'yes', her welcoming of God's choice of her, caused her to open herself, her whole life, her very womb; and she became the pivotal point of God's entering into human history. She opened up to the immensity of it; the grace which welcomes us as we are, revealing to our delirious joy that we are the objects of God's love. God's delight is in us. 'God's regard has made me great', she sings in her *Magnificat.*

---

12. From *Look to the Glory*, by Fr Richard M. Benson, Father Founder of the Society of Saint John the Evangelist.

13. From 'Advent' by Jessica Powers, in *Selected Poetry of Jessica Powers*, Regina Siegfried, A.S.C., and Robert F. Morneau, Sheed and Ward, 1989, p. 81.

Her response of welcome to God's taking initiative in her life was a total giving of body and soul

In the same way, our response involves our offering of our physical reality to Love. Our dwelling in God's welcome means we become available to one another as well as to God in bodily presence. Within a culture which both idolises and degrades the human body, this is so important. The body as the instrument of God's grace, the vehicle of God's message of love, expresses a deep truth about our nature and shows us how confused we have become. In community, the regular acts of worshipping and eating together strengthen the corporate life through their physical reality as well as their spiritual meaning. Living closely with one another in community, one is very much aware of the power of our physical reality. It is both a great source of strength and a challenge –because of what we communicate, consciously or otherwise, through our body language.

CARRIERS OF JOY

We are all created to carry joy into the world: the joy of responding to God's initiative in our lives. This joy can only occur, however, where God is given the freedom to be God. For religious, the vows taken are the enabling gift for this to happen, because they set us free from the need for success and control so that God's joy can manifest itself.[14]

To be carriers of joy suggests something important about the nature of our minds: that they are primarily receptive rather than controlling. Iain Matthew, O.C.D., explores this theme in the writings of St John of the Cross:

The mind does achieve, attain, but for John, the mind's deepest characteristic is its ability to receive, to welcome, to let in … To understand is above all to receive a light. How willing is my mind to let itself be bathed in another's light? … What opposes the mind's receptivity is the dominance of my own criteria as I look out

14. Archbishop Rowan Williams stressed this at the millennium gathering of Anglican Religious, at Hayes Conference Centre, Swanwick, September 2000.

on the world. Spirit is the person at the level of deepest welcome.[15]

As with God, so in our relationships with one another, we need to give space to allow for the gift of Love, unexpected and unplanned-for though its arrival will be. Profound encounters with other people can play a significant role on our journey into Love's welcome. We can all think of particular relationships which have opened the eyes of our hearts and drawn us, albeit sometimes painfully, out of our protective selves and into more authentic and sensitive relating with others. Such encounters open the heart to the promise of union with God and, in God, with the whole of creation. As we wait for the full consummation of this promise, it is important that we don't cling to the experiences of love, but allow them to point us towards a greater freedom in God.

> He who binds to himself a joy
> Does the winged life destroy;
> But he who kisses the joy as it flies
> Lives in eternity's sun rise.[16]

The Rule of our community contains a passage on the vow of chastity which illuminates this theme:

Chastity implies the right ordering of imagination, emotions and all creative energies. It gathers up the whole world of human relationships, all marriages, friendships and loyalties, all instincts of desire, tenderness and self-giving, into the marriage union of Christ with his Church.[17]

The second sentence describes the drawing of all human relational energies into the dynamic of Christ's incarnation and resurrection and ongoing work of redemption through human beings.

---

15. From an article, 'St John of the Cross and the Seasons of Prayer: III Anointing the Mind', by Iain Matthew, O.C.D.; in *Mount Carmel*, Autumn 2000, published by the Teresian Carmelites of the Anglo-Irish Province.
16. William Blake, 'Eternity', in *Poems*, Thomas Nelson and Sons Ltd., London, p. 192.
17. From the *Rule of the Society of the Sacred Cross*, Revised 1978, Tymawr Convent Press, Lydart, Monmouth.

LOVE CREATES COMMUNITY

In human relationships of intimacy, there is a gradual letting go of self-concern and separateness, to explore together. This is necessary, for a greater reality to be born. This dynamic must surely be part of the dynamic of love amongst the three Persons of the Trinity. If communities are called to mirror this flow of love, we too need to let go of some of the sense of 'my' identity so that a greater identity can be discovered amongst us. When, for example, we experience conflict with another in community, are we prepared to 'give our shirt as well as our coat'?[18] In other words, rather than retreating with our own judgements of the other as being totally separate from us, are we willing to relinquish another level of our self-protection, trusting that enfolding it all is the reality of Love which unites? Jesus teaches his followers that the 'good news' he has brought to the world requires a stripping away of limits: where one is called to love and pray for those whom we find antagonistic, to give without measuring or expecting a return, to 'go the extra mile'; for this is to reflect God's love. It involves moving beyond our familiar frames of reference and ways of doing things.

But letting go of self-defences in order to meet the 'other' (including the unreconciled places within ourselves) is possible only in the knowledge of God's welcome of us, which holds us secure in who we are, and gives us the confidence to move towards the other in this welcome of Love. In other words, we need to let God's love do the moving or drawing. Another's truth is always held in the love and truth of God. Here is one example of where praying for each other is so important. Acknowledging another in God's presence sheds light on our perspective of them, and enables grace to flow within the relationship. If we're willing, Love can and will create something new.

St Benedict reveals in his Rule that our salvation in community is not an individual affair – our seeking of and responding to Christ, first and foremost, in those with whom we live is our salvation. Christ is

18. Lk 6:29

found in the reality of our relationships. There is a story told of a man who visited a monastery and noticed how cold the monks were towards one another. He let it be known to the Abbot that Jesus himself was due to come and visit them. This news spread like wildfire around the monastery and the monks began to anticipate his visit. Their expectation of Jesus' arrival had a strange effect upon their relationships with one another. Not knowing whether Jesus had already arrived, as he would no doubt come incognito, they became much more aware of how they treated one another. A short while later, the man returned to the monastery and was amazed at the different atmosphere that greeted him. Jesus had indeed come among them. Thomas Merton used to tell his novices to concentrate on looking for Christ in one another, rather than being preoccupied with whether others could see him in them.

Learning to accept one another 'warts and all' is fundamental to living in community. Soon after arriving, as the dust begins to settle, one finds that these people one is living with have quirks and chipped corners like anybody else! This can be a great eye-opener and source of healing – after some initial feeling of disillusionment. Most importantly, it allows one to see God, whose grace is working through each member and through the community as a whole. One begins to experience the presence of God in the space which opens up through this way of living and in the very ordinariness of our shared life. Because of the frailty of human nature, we need to hold ourselves and one another gently, in God, and if possible with a chuckle!

LOVE SEEKS US IN THE SHADOWS

We need to keep open the place of questioning within us. The Virgin Mary, like us in her humanity and gradual growth in understanding, 'pondered in her heart' all the things that were happening to her. She must have had fears and questions, held the tension of the different opinions of others, and so lived with the unfolding of God's purposes in her daily life. And in the meantime, as with us, in the space within her, the Christ-child was growing.

The unresolved conflicts and questions in our own lives can also be places of welcome if we allow them to speak to us. Mother Rosemary, S.L.G.,[19] has spoken about the importance of these 'gaps', within and between us, in our lives together in community. If we don't try to close them too soon, but hear what they are saying to us, even when it means facing fear and the less 'civilised' parts of ourselves, we can receive profound insights, new vision and growth. These gaps within and amongst us can hold differences and unresolved tensions. We are naturally tempted to hunt for familiarity when sometimes we need to accept that we are in new territory, where perhaps a new language needs uncovering. There are times when we need to keep silent rather than rush into speech, and make space for the flow of tears. We can be premature with our forgiveness, replacing true forgiveness with hypocrisy, 'a pretence to forgive', a 'forgiving too soon'.

All illumination casts shadow. The deeper and sharper the shadow, the closer it is to the illuminated object. So, shadow can guide us and reveal to us where the illumination is. Our own shadow, that part of us which has been marginalised, which exists 'on the edge' of how we see ourselves, is not therefore something we move away from as we journey towards God. If anything, the shadow is likely to become deeper, sharper and less penetrable. We need to allow ourselves to experience the love of God penetrating this less manageable and acceptable part of ourselves. Our shadow can show us much, including places within us which are not free and still feel unloved and caught by the need for affirmation from others. When faced with it, we can challenge the fear which has us in its grip and allow God to show us that love holds us safe; that our security is not based on what others think of us, or even our opinion of ourselves, but the steadfast love of God which does not ebb and flow.

Thinking again of the contrast in welcome between the 'sinners' of Jesus' day and the religious leaders who couldn't receive him, I am aware of the possible place of shadow in their differing responses. The contrast seems to be between those who saw in Love personified in

19. From an address given at the millennium gathering of Anglican Religious, September 2000.

Jesus a welcome, and those who perceived it as a threat, letting their fear distort reality. Were the 'sinners' drawn to Christ because they were aware of their need, weakness and shadow, and let it reveal Love's presence to them? In contrast, could the religious leaders, perhaps, not admit or own their shadow and weakness, finding the invitation to freedom offered by Love a threat, and so projecting onto Jesus what they couldn't cope with in themselves? The story told in the Gospels of the tax collector and the Pharisee in the Temple [20] can be read in this light. One, the tax collector, recognises the healing power of love, while the other is trapped in judgement, refusing to own his brokenness and shadow, and projecting it onto others.

A lot of our journeying together in community seems to be tied up with how we 'manage' shadow. If we are all travelling towards the light, we are inevitably going to meet in shadow. We're bound to bump into one another a bit in the dark! God accepts and loves our corporate shadow as much as our 'light': in fact, as Isaiah writes, God promises us, 'I will give you the treasures of darkness'.[21] The challenge may be to not hide from this beautiful reality; it can allow God to bring us much closer together in trust and love.

Can we live creatively with our own and others' shadows, in the light of God's acceptance and love of it all, trusting that we are not asked to be other than we are, but just to live fully and confidently what we are? We know the factions and polarities that inevitably result from a refusal to own anger and 'negative' emotions. Even wars can be traced to human inability to channel these emotions. As St Paul warns the group of Christians in Ephesus to whom he writes, 'In your anger, do not sin'.[22] It's not the anger that is the problem; it's whether we're prepared to work with it and allow it to be a force for good, for positive growth, rather than let ourselves give in to the temptation to simply 'go with it'. The religious vow of obedience, involving a mutual listening and responding to the Spirit at work in a community, can encompass this challenge. Are we prepared to allow the whole of

20. Lk 18:9-14
21. Is 45:3
22. Eph 4:26.

ourselves to become a part of the 'spiritual temple' God builds with us as a community?

DYING INTO NEW LIFE

One of the Eucharistic Prayers [23] includes the words, 'On the Cross he opened wide his arms of mercy, embracing us in perfect love, destroying the power of evil, suffering and death'. Christ's welcome to us involved his death: a total giving of self, total surrender. It was for Jesus the moment of greatest desolation. The next words in the prayer reveal the consequences and immense power of this surrender of Love: 'On the first day of the week you raised him from the dead and opened to us the gate of everlasting life'. This total giving into the hands of the One he called Father enabled Jesus to offer this eternal welcome for the whole of creation into the very life of God.

In community, there is a dying to our isolated sense of identity and into new corporate life, the risen life of Christ: 'unless a grain of wheat falls into the ground and dies, it remains but a single grain; but if it dies, it produces many grains'.[24] Our welcome is rooted in the death and resurrection of Christ. For the Society of the Sacred Cross, the Cross is experienced profoundly as the place where we are all gathered and held in love. It is the place where Christian community began; the place where Jesus revealed new family ties between his mother and his closest disciple: 'and from that time on, this disciple took her into his home'.[25] It is also the place where a vocation – the realisation of God's purpose for one' s life – begins, as the foot of the Cross is the place where we experience most deeply God's welcome and our ability to welcome one another in the light of this.

THE ECONOMY OF LOVE

The Gospels record an occasion when, whilst the disciples were travelling along on the road – which can be a symbol for us of our

---

23. From *An Alternative Order for the Holy Eucharist*, Church in Wales Publications, 1994.
24. Jn 12:24
25. Jn 19:27

journeying together – they were competing with one another for status. Jesus responded by focussing their minds on welcome, the welcome of a little child whom he set in their midst. He explained to them that by welcoming such a child they were in fact welcoming God, the One who alone could fulfil their deepest hopes. We can afford to make room for each other in the economy of Love because there is no rationing or shortage. The more competitive we are, the less open we shall be to this truth about love, and the more defensive we shall become. In this way, we lose the sense that God loves and welcomes us as we are. Competitiveness reveals a lack of faith in our intrinsic worth as human beings, and a belief that one's worth depends on 'coming out better' when comparing oneself with another.

Jesus teaches his followers that love reverses human value systems which are built on competition and comparison. That which is weak in the world's eyes, in the light of our competitive ways of living and seeing the world, rests in God's reality, in the knowledge that we are all dependent on God and all of infinite worth. That within us which feels most vulnerable often holds the deepest wisdom and is the most clear-sighted. We tend to know 'in our bones' that it is not in our strength that we meet one another, but in our solidarity as fellow human beings in our struggle and fragility.

Religious communities can witness to this understanding of love through their corporate life in which a competitive way of living, where power rules the day, has been laid aside. This enables religious communities to point to the greater reality of love in which all have a place and within which there is no partiality. It is not by virtue of their gifts, abilities or character that each member belongs to the community, nor because they have been chosen in preference to another. This is a strong witness in a world where people are seen to a large extent as commodities and the sense of community for its own sake has to a large extent disappeared. This aspect of religious communities can speak of the intrinsic worth of a person in a society where people have to fight to belong and to have an identity separate from their credentials. Visitors to religious communities find themselves welcomed for who they are, not for what they might represent. This is often a very healing experience for people, enabling the relaxing of self-imposed identities and allowing the true person to flourish.

LEARNING TO BE CHILD-LIKE

Jesus warns his followers that unless they are prepared to receive the Kingdom of God as a child, they will never enter it. Our judgement of others blocks off our openness to receive. It is frighteningly easy to label others as being a certain way and so to close off our ability to learn more deeply about them and to witness growth and change in them, and importantly, in ourselves. We are hindered in our freedom to welcome others as they are by needs within ourselves which at some point in our lives have been judged to be unacceptable, and so remain hidden and unmet. We may even be unaware of them, until Love's welcome draws them out into the light.

Learning to be real is part of learning to be child-like. It is learning to trust that our real needs can be met by Love. Indeed, they are the only place where Love can meet us, as the accounts of Jesus' healing in the Gospels show clearly. By owning and exploring them, we find both the God who is deeply with us and solidarity with others sharing the human journey. We're still on the way; we're not there yet. Our needs and unfulfilled desires reveal to us that we're journeying ever more deeply into Love.

This – the non-judgemental transparency of the hearts which we begin with as children and need to re-learn – also creates a deeper communion between us, as it opens us to recognise and respond to Love's welcome in one another. There is, for example, in the story of the woman who anointed Jesus' feet, [26] a mutual welcoming between the woman and Jesus. They are humbly receiving from one another, each serving the other in love and trust. The story speaks to me of what service is all about: true meeting and mutual welcoming. Service involves the willingness to receive the generosity and hospitality of another, as well as to provide it. In many churches and religious

26. Lk 7:36-50.

houses at a special service on Maundy Thursday there is a re-enactment of the washing of the disciples' feet by Jesus during his Last Supper with them. This serving of one another in a symbolic way can be a very powerful experience as we take time over, and express our care for another.

The woman's encounter with Jesus causes her to weep and fall at his feet, revealing another important aspect of God' s welcome. Jesus contrasts the response of Simon, the host, with hers: 'The one who has been forgiven little loves little'. She was open to the divinity of Jesus touching her inner knowledge of her need for the healing love and mercy of God. Religious life includes within it a strong element of repentance, of continual turning and re-turning to God. Rather than overemphasising human sinfulness, it reveals the ability and per-petual desire of God to heal and uphold us, and our relationships with one another. Like a constant turning towards the light and warmth of the sun, it acknowledges the source of our life and renewal, and gives rise to deep thankfulness.

A significant proportion of the Psalms that religious regularly recite in the daily Offices express this constant returning to God. The saying of the Psalms is on behalf, not only of the Church, but the whole of humankind, and therefore there is, in reality, a continual turning towards God by the human race. It is therefore a crucial part of the intercession that religious communities offer on behalf of the world. The Psalms express the whole range of human emotion and experi-ence, and so there is a gathering up into the Love of God of the whole reality of humanity with the cyclical reciting of the Psalter.

LISTENING WITH AN OPEN HEART

Mary's amazement at God's choice of her leads to boldness and confidence and prophetic utterance. In her *Magnificat*, she speaks of God's purposes of 'raising up the poor' and 'filling the hungry with good things'. God's welcome is unexpected, meeting and addressing the deepest needs of a vulnerable humanity, cutting through pretence and human-made oppressive structures to free human beings to rejoice in their Maker.

The Gospel accounts of the woman anointing Jesus' head are placed on both occasions [27] at one of the most significant points in Jesus' life: just before his passion and death. It has been pointed out how prophetic and bold this gesture was as, according to Jewish custom, to perform this action was to anoint Jesus as Prophet, King and High Priest. As with the other accounts, the woman's actions led to scorn and moral condemnation from those around, who complained of the huge waste of money. And as with the other accounts, Jesus' response is in contrast with this. He says, 'She has done a beautiful thing to me ... she did it to prepare me for burial.' He declared the immense significance of her actions with the words, 'I tell you the truth, wherever this gospel is preached throughout the world, what she has done will also be told, in memory of her.'

Can our welcome be prophetic too? The woman who anointed Jesus' head, unidentified, without importance in the eyes of all present apart from Jesus, perceived in Jesus what few had; and more than this, was prepared to declare what she had perceived.

The message here seems to be primarily about our willingness to listen to what is going on around and within with openness, and being prepared to be moved to act upon it. Our conscious mind is so full of agendas and pre-taped messages. We spend so much of our time in a closed reality. Listening with an open heart is a way through into hearing the Spirit. We need to be ready to welcome. Jesus speaks often about this to his followers, usually in vivid stories which will capture their imagination, such as the parable of the ten virgins, half of whom kept their lamps trimmed and were ready to greet the bridegroom when he arrived.[28] He constantly reminds them that the arrival of God is unexpected, and so we need to keep aware and attentive. St Benedict begins his *Rule for Monks* with the word, 'listen', and quoting from Psalm 95, he admonishes them not to harden their hearts. Henri Caffarel writes:

27. Mt 26:6-13; Mk 14:3-9.
28. Mt 25:1-13

[the word] 'listen' indicates not a solitary activity but a meeting, an exchange, between one heart and another: which is the essence of prayer.[29]

Obedience is part of the necessary fabric of the religious life, of life in community. The Latin phrase from which it comes is *'Ob Audire'* which means 'to listen'. Therefore, at its root obedience is about listening: listening together to the Spirit at the heart of things. Trusting in one another in this way is both life-giving and life-creating, though costly.

Obedience is also about recognising that I can't make it on my own. We find others come into our lives who, we recognise, are there to help and guide us, and we need to acknowledge their authority. In community, we are provided both with a specific guide in the formative years, with the leader of the community who has received the grace to be a focal point for the Spirit's guidance, and the other members of the community, who have been trusted with the task of discerning together the will of God for the ongoing life of the community.

Real choice involves making decisions which limit our apparent freedom. Listening to God is always an invitation to deeper freedom. A prayer often used by the Church contains the phrase, 'whose service is perfect freedom', referring to God. True freedom is not about unlimited choice, but awareness of choice made freely and responsibly. Mary's choice to accept God's invitation closed off particular avenues to her and opened immense possibilities of love and pain. Our welcome of God also involves our journeying into the unknown: but as the saying goes, 'I may not know what tomorrow holds, but I know the One who holds tomorrow.' All we are asked to do is trust.

LOVE'S CREATIVITY

Made in the image of the Creator, it must be that our creativity is a fundamental part of our humanity, and so part of our sharing in Love's welcome together. By this I mean our exploring and express-

29. From *Presence a Dieu*, Edit. du Feu nouveau, Paris, 1970, pp. 130-132.

ing of aspects of our inner and outer landscape through various media such as music, visual art, movement and clay. Activities such as cooking and writing can also be very creative. The wonder is when we find that what is expressed connects with others. Somehow the very act of creating, and often the creation itself, can become 'walking space' for others, and the experience can be enlarging as it is shared. Whether it is finding one's heart touched and opened by a moving piece of poetry or music, or discovering shared ground when singing, dancing or enjoying nature together, we know within that our humanity has been deepened.

'Love alone is creative,' said Maximilian Kolbe.[30] The dynamic perceived in creative expression appears to be remarkably similar to that of Love. There is an 'opening up', a 'reaching out', an 'outpouring', and seen vividly in movement and dance, a 'stretching out' which has always struck me in the position of Jesus, Love personified, on the Cross. There is a vulnerability about the creative process which is that of Love, and the need for inner yielding and gentleness. Maybe this is part of the creating of a space which can be shared with others. And the bonding of shared experience and meaning creates community between people.

Love's welcome is a place both of stillness and of movement: 'Except for the point, the still point, there would be no dance, and there is only the dance.'[31] As such, it reflects the three Persons of the Trinity, who are gathered and yet in motion. There is both arrival and journey, holding and releasing, similarity and difference. It is also a place of both joy and suffering. The reality of the Cross is at the heart of the Trinity, revealing that the love of God does not exist or flow independent of suffering. All pain is gathered up into the very life of God and thus transformed into something creative: God sharing his life with us. Pain can create a place into which we can welcome others who are suffering. Those who have suffered a particular loss are usually the

30. Polish saint and martyr during the Nazi regime.
31. T.S. Eliot, in 'Burnt Norton' from the 'Four Quartets', in *The Complete Poems and Plays of T.S. Eliot*, Faber and Faber, London, 1969.

best equipped to help others in a similar situation and often feel drawn to do so.

> Prayer is letting one's own heart become the place where the tears of God and the tears of God's children can merge and become tears of hope.[32]

It is the miracle of the cry of humanity, the primal cry, being voiced and heard in us, through our acknowledging that very cry in the depths of our own being.

The dwelling in Love is a dwelling in vulnerability, where we are relying on the grace of God which He has promised will be 'sufficient for us'.[33] The landscape is unfamiliar and perhaps unclear: our eyes unaccustomed to this way of seeing as we learn to see with the eyes of faith. It is a place where everything is turned upside down, and we become aware of the reality of things beneath what we are used to: where foolishness undermines wisdom as we know it, and weakness, strength. A place of good news, 'Gospel', because we are shown that we are not the ultimate end of things, God is: the God who created out of nothing and alone has the power to reduce to nothing. So, new ways open up to us as we become accustomed to this new way of seeing: freedom, communion, the mysterious, untraceable ways of Love. It is the place where God's love is seen as the initiator of all.

———————

Our response, as individually we encounter the reality of Love, necessarily draws us into relationship with Love. This relationship undergirds all our human relationships and draws us into authentic encounters with others, where we can truly meet without the games of power we so often get caught up in. God leads us deeper into the reality of love as we learn to listen to him and to one another. Love calls us on in its welcome: enabling us to risk letting go of our grip on the things which give us security, our self-image, our need for attention

32. Henri Nouwen, *Seeds of Hope*, Darton, Longman and Todd, London, 1989, p. 68.
33. 2 Cor 12:9.

and to possess and control others. It calls us into a space, a reality, which we don't control but rather that holds us in its embrace, and within which we find the whole of creation is held too. Love alone can heal. It casts out the fear which cripples us and bestows the gift of trust. Orthodox Christianity teaches us to rest the mind in the heart, the place where trust can grow. This life of Love into which we are called is the life of Christ himself, drawing us ever deeper into the very heart of the life of the Trinity – the relationship of infinite love which is God.

> Praise to God, our saving Wisdom,
> Meeting us with love and grace,
> Helping us to grow in wholeness,
> Giving freedom, room and space …
>
> In our searching, In our loving,
> In our struggles to be free,
> God is present, living in us,
> Pointing us to what shall be.[34]

---

34. From 'Praise to God the World's Creator' by Jan Berry, in *Celebrating Women*, ed. Ward, Wild and Morley, SPCK, London, 1995, p. 138..

Select Bibliography

HISTORIES OF COMMUNITIES, AND BIOGRAPHIES
OF FOUNDERS AND PROMINENT MEMBERS

All Saints Sisters of the Poor
Peter Mayhew, *All Saints: Birth and Growth of a Community,* ASSP, Oxford, 1987.
Susan Mumm (editor), *All Saints Sisters of the Poor: an Anglican Sisterhood in the Nineteenth Century,* Boydell Press, Woodbridge, 2001.

Brotherhood of the Ascended Christ
Constance M Millington, *Whether We Be Many or Few: a History of the Cambridge / Delhi Brotherhood,* Asian Trading Corporation, Bangalore, 1999.

Brotherhood and Sisterhood of the Epiphany,
and the Christa Sevika Sangha
Brethren of the Epiphany, *A Hundred Years in Bengal,* ISPCK, Delhi, 1979.
G. Wilson (ed.), *Theodore: Letters from the Oxford Mission in India, 1946–1993,* Oxford Mission, Romsey, 1997.
Sister Leonore CSF, *Journeying On,* Churchman, Worthing, 1990.
Sister Rosamund SE, *He Leadeth Me: Memoirs of an Oxford Sister of the Epiphany,* Oxford Mission, Romsey, 1999.
Mother Susila CSS, *A Well Watered Garden,* (editor: M Pickering), Oxford Mission, Romsey, 2000.

Christa Seva Sangha / Christa Prema Seva Sangha
Jack Winslow, *The Eyelids of the Dawn,* Hodder and Stoughton, London, 1954.
Sister Barbara Noreen CSMV, A *Wheat Grain Sown in India,* privately published, 1988.

— —, *Crossroads of the Spirit,* ISPCK, Delhi, 1994.

Community of All Hallows
Sister Violet CAH, *All Hallows, Ditchingham,* Becket Publications, Oxford, 1983.
Mother Mary CAH, *Memories,* All Hallows, Ditchingham, 1998.

Community of the Holy Cross
Alan Russell, *The Community of the Holy Cross Haywards Heath 1857–1957: a Short History of its Life and Work,* Holy Cross Convent, Haywards Heath, 1957.

Community of the Holy Family
Community of the Holy Family, *Community of the Holy Family: the First Sixty Years, 1898-1958,* privately produced by the community.

Community of the Holy Name (founded in Australia)
Sister Elizabeth CHN, *Esther, Mother Foundress,* Melbourne, 1948.
Lynn Strahan, *Out of the Silence,* OUP, Melbourne, 1988.

Community of the Holy Name (founded in the UK)
History of the Community of the Holy Name, 1865 to 1950, Community of the Holy Name, Malvern, 1950.
Una C. Hannam, *Portrait of a Community,* printed by the Church Army Press, Malvern, 1972.

Community of the Holy Spirit
Mother Ruth CHS, *In Wisdom Thou hast made them,* Adams, Bannister & Cox, New York, 1986.

Community of Jesus of Nazareth
Margaret Duggan, *The Convent of the Sisters of the Community of Jesus of Nazareth, Westcote,* Westcote Historical Society, Westcote, 1993.
Kenneth Packard, *Brother Edward: Priest and Evangelist,* Bles, London, 1955

Community of the Resurrection

Alan Wilkinson, *The Community of the Resurrection: A Centenary History,* SCM Press, London, 1992.

G. L. Prestige, *The Life of Charles Gore: a Great Englishman,* Heinemann, London, 1935.

C. S. Phillips, *Walter Howard Frere, Bishop of Truro,* Faber & Faber, London, 1947.

Nicholas Mosley, *Raymond Raynes,* Faith Press, London, 1961.

G. P. H. Pawson (compiler), *Edward Keble Talbot,* SPCK, London, 1954.

Robin Denniston, *Trevor Huddleston,* Macmillan, London, 1999.

Community of the Resurrection of Our Lord

A Sister of the Community (compiler), *Mother Cecile in South Africa 1883–1906: Foundress of the Community of the Resurrection of Our Lord,* SPCK, London, 1930.

A Sister of the Community, *The Story of a Vocation: a Brief Memoir of Mother Florence, Second Superior of the Community of the Resurrection of Our Lord,* The Church Book Shop, Grahamstown, no date.

Community of the Sacred Passion

Sister Mary Stella CSP, *She Won't Say 'No': The History of the Community of the Sacred Passion,* CSP, Effingham, 1984.

Community of St Denys

CSD: The Life & Work of St Denys, Warminster, Community of St Denys, Warminster, 1979.

Community of St Francis

Elizabeth CSF, *Corn of Wheat,* Becket Publications, Oxford, 1981.

Community of St John the Baptist

T. T. Carter, *Harriet Monsell: a Memoir,* J. Masters, London, 1886.

Valerie Bonham, *A Joyous Service: The Clewer Sisters and Their Work*, Community of St John the Baptist, Clewer, 1989.

————, *A Place in Life: The House of Mercy 1849-1883* , Community of St John the Baptist, Clewer, 1992.

————, *The Sisters of the Raj: The Clewer Sisters in India*, 1997.

James Simpson and Edward Story, *Stars in His Crown,* Ploughshare Press, Sea Bright, NJ, 1976.

Community of St Mary

Sister Mary Hilary CSM, *Ten Decades of Praise,* DeKoven Foundation, Racine, WI, 1965.

Community of St Mary the Virgin

A Hundred Years of Blessing, SPCK, London, 1946.

From Theatre to Convent: Memories of Mother Isabel Mary, SPCK, London, 1936.

Sister Janet CSMV, *Mother Maribel of Wantage,* SPCK, London, 1972.

Community of St Michael and All Angels

Margaret Leith, *One the Faith,* Community of St Michael and All Angels, Bloemfontein, 1971.

Mary Brewster, *One the Earnest Looking Forward,* Community of St Michael and All Angels, Bloemfontein, 1991.

Community of St Peter (Woking)

Elizabeth Cuthbert, *In St Peter's Shadow,* Community of St Peter, Woking, 1994.

Community of the Sisters of the Church

A Valiant Victorian: the Life and Times of Mother Emily Ayckbowm 1836-1900, of the Community of the Sisters of the Church, Mowbray, London, 1964.

Community of the Servants of the Will of God

R. D. Hacking, *Sucah a Long Journey: a Biography of Gilbert Shaw, Priest,* Mowbray, London, 1988.

Community of the Transfiguration

Mrs Harlan Cleveland, *Mother Eva Mary CT: The Story of a*

foundation, Morehouse, Milwaukee, WI, 1929.

Melanesian Brotherhood
Brian Macdonald Milne, *Spearhead: the Story of the Melanesian Brotherhood,* privately published.

Oratory of the Good Shepherd
George Tibbatts, *The Oratory of the Good Shepherd: The First Seventy-five Years,* Oratory of the Good Shepherd, Windsor, 1988.

Order of the Holy Cross
Adarn Dunbar McCoy OHC, *Holy Cross: a Century of Anglican Monasticism,* Morehouse-Barlow, Wilton, CT, 1987.
Vita Duddon Scudder, *Father Huntington: Founder of the Order of the Holy Cross,* E. P. Dutton, New York, 1940.
S. C Hughson, *An American Cloister,* Holy Cross Publications, New York, 1961.

Order of the Holy Paraclete
A Foundation Member, *Fulfilled in Joy,* Hodder & Stoughton, London, 1964.
Rosalin Barker, *The Whitby Sisters: a Chronicle of the Order of the Holy Paraclete, 1915-2000,* published by the Order of the Holy Paraclete, Whitby, 2001.

Order of Julian of Norwich
Teunisje Velthuizen, *One-ed into God: The First Decade of the Order of St Julian of Norwich,* The Julian Press, Waukesha, WI, 1996.

Order of St Benedict (Father Ignatius)
Baroness de Bertouch, *The Life of Father Ignatius OSB, Monk of Llanthony,* Methuen, London, 1904.
Arthur Calder-Marshall, *The Enthusiast*, Faber & Faber, London, 1962.

Order of St Benedict (Caldey Island)
Peter F. Anson, *The Benedictines of Caldey,* Catholic Book Club, London, 1940; revised ed: Prinknash Abbey, Prinknash, 1944.

Peter F. Anson, *Abbot Extraordinary,* Faith Press, London, 1958.

Order of St Benedict (Pershore, Nashdom, Elmore – UK)
The Jubilee Book of the Benedictines of Nashdom 1914-1964, Faith Press, London, 1964.

E. M. Almedingen, *Dom Bernard Clements: a Portrait,* John Lane, London, 1945.

Dom Anselm Hughes, *Rivers of the Flood,* Faith Press, London, 1961.

Simon Bailey, *A Tactful God: Gregory Dix,* Gracewing, Leominister, 1995.

Order of St Benedict (Three Rivers, Michigan – USA)
Singing God's Praises, Order of St Benedict, Three Rivers, MN, 1998.

Sisterhood of St John the Divine
Sister Eleonora SSJD, *A Memoir of the Life of and Work of Hannah Grier Coombe, Mother-Foundress of the Sisterhood of St John the Divine, Toronto, Canada,* Oxford University Press, London, 1933.

The Sisterhood of St John the Divine 1884-1984, published 1931 as *A Brief History;* fourth revision, Sisterhood of St John the Divine, Toronto, 1984.

Society of the Divine Compassion
A. Clifton Kelway, *A Franciscan Revival: The Story of the Society of the Divine Compassion,* Society of the Divine Compassion, London, 1908.

Kathleen E. Burne (editor), *The Life and Letters of Father Andrew SDC,* Mowbray, London, 1948.

Geoffrey Curtis, *William of Glasshampton: Friar, Monk, Solitary, 1862-1937,* SPCK, London, 1947.

Society of the Holy Cross
Jae Joung Lee, *Society of the Holy Cross 1925-1995,* Seoul, 1995 (in Korean).

Society of the Love of Jesus
E. D. Ward-Harris, A *Nun goes to the Dogs,* Collins, Toronto, 1969.

Society of the Precious Blood
Sister Felicity Mary SPB, *Mother Millicent Mary of the Will of God,* Macmillan, London, 1968.

Society of the Sacred Advent
Elizabeth Moores, *One Hundred Years of Ministry,* published for Society of the Sacred Advent, 1992.

Society of the Holy Trinity
T. J. Williams, *Priscilla Lydia Sellon,* SPCK, London, 1950.
T. J. Williams & A. W. Campbell, *The Park Village Sisterhood,* SPCK, London, 1965.

Society of the Sacred Mission
Alistair Mason, SSM, *History of the Society of the Sacred Mission,* Canterbury Press, Norwich, 1993.
Herbert H. Kelly SSM, *An Idea in the Working,* SSM Press, Kelham, 1908.
Herbert H. Kelly SSM, (edited by George Every SSM) *No Pious Person: Autobiographical Reflections,* Faith Press, London, 1960.
Michael Worsnip, *Priest and Partisan: a South African Journey,* Ocean Press, Melbourne, 1996.

Society of St Francis (& associated Franciscan communities)
Petà Dunstan, *This Poor Sort: A History of the European Province of the Society of Saint Francis,* Darton Longman and Todd, London, 1997.
Fr Francis SSF, *Brother Douglas. Apostle of the Outcast,* Mowbray, London, 1959.
Fr Denis, *Father Algy,* Hodder & Stoughton, London, 1964.
Br Kenneth SSF, *A Brother's Way: The Memoirs of Brother Kenneth SSF*, Society of St Francis Hilfield, 1991.
Br Michael Fisher SSF, *For the Time Being: a Memoir,* Gracewing,

Leominster, 1993.

Br Ramon SSF, *Franciscan Spirituality*, SPCK, London, 1994.

George Potter, *Father Potter of Peckham*, Hodder, London, 1955.

George Potter, *More Father Potter of Peckham*, Hodder, London, 1958.

Bernard Palmer, *Men of Habit: the Franciscan Ideal in Action*, Canterbury Press, London, 1994.

Barrie Williams, *The Franciscan Revival in the Anglican Communion*, Darton Longman and Todd, London, 1982.

Society of St John the Divine
Sister Margaret Anne SSJD, *What the World Counts Weakness*, Society of St John the Divine, Durban, 1987.

Society of St John the Evangelist
R. M. Benson, *The Followers of the Lamb*, Longman, Green and Co., London, 1900.

———, *The Religious Vocation*, Mowbray, London, 1939.

———, *Letters of Richard Meux Benson*, Mowbray, London 1916.

———, *Further Letters of Richard Meux Benson*, Mowbray, London, 1920.

M. V. Woodgate, *Father Benson: Founder of the Cowley Fathers*, Bles, London 1953.

Martin Smith SSJE (editor), *Benson of Cowley*, Oxford University Press, Oxford, 1980.

John Nias, *Flame from an Oxford Cloister: The Life and Writings of Philip Napier Waggett*, Faith Press, London, 1961.

H. E. W. Slade, A *Work Begun: The Cowley Fathers in India 1874-1967*, SPCK, London, 1970.

Sisters of St Margaret
Sister Catherine Louise SSM, *The House of My Pilgrimage: a History of the American House of the Society of St Margaret*, privately published, 1973.

Sister Catherine Louise SSM, *The Planting of the Lord: the History of the Society of Saint Margaret in England, Scotland and the USA;*

privately published, 1995.

Pamela Myers, *Building for the Future: A Nursing History 1896 to 1996 to Commemorate the Centenary of St Mary's Convent and Nursing Home, Chiswick,* St Mary's Convent, Chiswick, 1996.

Doing the Impossible: a Short Sketch of St Margaret's Convent, East Grinstead 1855-1980, privately published, 1984.

Mother Kate, *Memories of a Sister of S. Saviour's Priory,* A.R. Mowbray, London, 1904.

Mother Kate, *Old Soho Days,* Mowbray, London, 1906.

A Hundred Years in Haggerston, St Saviour's Priory, London, 1966.

GENERAL HISTORIES AND STUDIES, AND BOOKS CONTAINING INFORMATION ON MORE THAN ONE COMMUNITY

Anglican Religious Communities Year Book 2004-2005, Canterbury Press, Norwich, 2003.

A. M. Allchin, *The Silent Rebellion,* SCM Press, London, 1958.

Peter F. Anson, *The Call of the Cloister: Religious Communities and Kindred Bodies in the Anglican Communion,* SPCK, London, 1955; revised edition 1964.

Allan T. Cameron, *The Religious Communities of the Church of England,* Faith Press, London, 1918.

H. Collett, *Little Gidding and its Founder,* SPCK, London, 1925.

Sister Edna Mary CSA, *The Religious Life,* Penguin, Harmondsworth, 1968.

Alan Harrison, *Bound for Life,* Mowbray, London, 1983.

M. Hill, *The Religious Order,* Heinemann, London, 1973.

Journey to God: Anglican Essays in the Benedictine Way, Malling Abbey, West Malling, 1980.

Isobel Losada, *New Habits,* Hodder & Stoughton, London, 1999.

Susan Mumm, *Stolen Daughters, Virgin Mothers,* Leicester University Press, Leicester, 1999.

A. Perchenet, *Religious Life and Christian Unity,* London, 1969.

Contributors

Alistair ssf was professed in the Society of St Francis in 1986. As a friar, he trained as a clinical psychologist, and is currently working with people with severe and enduring mental illness.

Annaliese csc has been a member of the Community of the Sisters of the Church for twelve years and has lived at their inner city house in St Paul's, Bristol for eight years.

Dr Petà Dunstan is the academic librarian of the Faculty of Divinity in the University of Cambridge, where she teaches modern Church history, and is a Fellow of St Edmund's College. She researches and lectures on the history of religious life, with particular reference to Anglican communities. She is the author of *This Poor Sort*, a history of the Society of St Francis.

Emma ssc is a junior professed member of the Society of the Sacred Cross, the core community of which lives a contemplative life of prayer in the borderlands of South Wales.

Gillian Ruth csmv was born in Yorkshire of a Methodist family. She became an Anglican at the age of twenty-five, and has been a member of the Community of St Mary the Virgin since 1982. She has had a ministry of retreat-giving and spiritual accompaniment for fifteen years, and is currently studying Christian spirituality at Heythrop College, University of London and lives in the community's house in north London.

Hilary ohp was educated by the Order of the Holy Paraclete at St Hilda's School, Whitby. After further education she made her profession in the Order in 1963. Since then she has experienced many aspects of the Order's life in England and Africa.

Nicolas cr is a Zimbabwean-born member of the Community of the Resurrection, Mirfield. His ministry is divided between retreat work, ecumenical contact and teaching in a theological college.

Richard MBH is an English-born member of the Melanesian Brotherhood who worked in Indonesia before ordination. He has particular interest in drama, and served as chaplain and teacher to the Brotherhood before joining them as a brother.

Stephanie Thérèse SLG is an American sister in the contemplative community of the Love of God, Fairaces, Oxford. Her delight in the Community is to cook for her sisters, when she gets the chance.

rlr RELIGIOUS LIFE REVIEW

Religious Life Review is a journal whose policy, since its first appearance in 1963, has been 'to provide a forum concentrating on problems of religious life or on questions which, though of interest to other Christians, might usefully be discussed in a more limited context.'

Religious Life Review appears six times a year.

Religious Life Review is published by

Dominican Publications

42 PARNELL SQUARE, DUBLIN 1, IRELAND

Fax +353-(0)1-873-1760

Email subscriptions@dominicanpublications.com